Untold Story of the INDIAN PUBLIC SECTOR

Untold Story of the INDIAN PUBLIC SECTOR

Dr. U.D. Choubey

STERLING PUBLISHERS PRIVATE LIMITED
Regd. Office: A-59, Okhla Industrial Area, Phase-II,
New Delhi-110020. CIN: U22110PB1964PTC002569
Tel: 26387070, 26386209; Fax: 91-11-26383788
E-mail: mail@sterlingpublishers.com
www.sterlingpublishers.com

Untold Story of the INDIAN PUBLIC SECTOR

ISBN 978 81 207 8832 9

Printed in India

Printed and Published by Sterling Publishers Pvt. Ltd.,
New Delhi-110 020.

Dedicated to my wife, Gita,
&
Mohit, Snigdha, Smriti & Kaiyra

Mani Shankar Aiyar
MEMBER OF PARLIAMENT
(RAJYA SABHA)

12, Safdarjung Lane
New Delhi -110 011
Tel. : 011-23795402
E-mail: manirsmp@gmail.com

Foreword

It has been my privilege to have known Dr. U.D. Choubey since he was Director in the Gas Authority of India Limited (GAIL) during the brief period that I served as Union Minister of Petroleum and Natural Gas (May 2004 - January 2006). As such, I should have been a target of attack by Dr. Choubey in this utterly frank and straightforward book. I am, therefore, deeply flattered that he should be asking me to write this Foreword. I am delighted to do so because I hold Dr. Choubey in high esteem.

The high point of my brief tenure was Cabinet approving in February 2005 my proposal that we open negotiations with Pakistan and Iran for laying a pipeline from the Gulf coast of Iran to Rajasthan through Pakistan to import a very large quantity of natural gas to fuel our nation's energy security, without which there is no prospect of our breaking into double-digit growth figures, as was the expectation at that time. Of course GAIL played a major role in preparing us for that break-through project as well as assisting me in the first few rounds of negotiations. It was during this time that Dr. Choubey made a deep impression on me with his understanding of the broad politico-economic context of the negotiations as well as the technical details. Unfortunately, the combination of the endeavour to secure an Indo-US nuclear deal to pull the country out of the nuclear apartheid in which we had been fenced since the Pokharan-2 explosions of May 1988 and the Iran-Libya Sanctions Act (ILSA) passed by the US legislature several years earlier resulted in the initiative being virtually aborted almost as soon as it started. But the sterling preparatory work done by GAIL, to which Dr. Choubey made a significant contribution, remains on record and will prove invaluable whenever India turns to its only real source of succour which is the vast natural gas deposits of Iran that we can access by pipeline without having to convert it into LNG.

Soon after I was asked to step down from the Ministry, Dr. Choubey became the Chairman of GAIL and continued to keep me informed of the country's energy problems and GAIL's contribution to meeting our requirements of hydrocarbons. It was also a period in which GAIL diversified and became increasingly involved with the petroleum industry instead of being confined to the laying and maintenance of pipelines.

....2

My association with Dr. Choubey continued with perhaps even more vigour when, on retirement from GAIL, he became the Director General of the Standing Conference of Public Enterprises (SCOPE) and we were together able to explore horizons that went beyond, but included, the petroleum industry. I have long been acquainted with SCOPE but I saw it taking new wings under the direction of Dr. Choubey.

The present book introduces us to his life story which is equally as fascinating as that of others who make a political virtue of their humble origins. In Dr. Choubey's case, however, these humble origins have been transformed into the service of the nation in a highly techno-managerial sector and in defence of the usually denigrated public sector that Pandit Jawaharlal Nehru had conceived as the bulwark of the nation's industry and infrastructure. The "modern temples of India" were to be erected by the public sector.

Dr. Choubey details what went wrong with that noble idea in the process of implementation. One cannot but regret that too many of Panditji's successors failed to live up to his noble vision. Dr. Choubey's rise to the higher echelons of the public sector coincided with the deliberate denigration and even gradual dismantlement of our public sector enterprises. Dr. Choubey explains how this need not have necessarily been so. Even now, if his prescriptions are listened to, the public sector can re-emerge as a giant on its own, competing with the private sector and yet serving larger national goals than merely propping up the bottom-line of a balance sheet.

His systematic exposition of what he calls the "Untold Story" of our Public Sector Enterprises is, therefore, especially timely and, if taken seriously, could lead to that resurgence in PSEs which might yet pull us out of the current stagnation in manufacturing that is sucking into quicksand our hopes of making our country prosperous and ensuring remunerative employment to the millions of young men and women who are joining the ranks of those seeking to contribute to the building of our modern nation.

I extend to Dr. Choubey my warmest congratulations and my deep gratitude for having allowed me to write this Foreward - even though I sat opposite him on the other side of the table!

(Mani Shankar Aiyar)

New Delhi.
31 January 2014

Preface

During my 37 years of service in the Indian Public Sector and five years in SCOPE (Standing Conference of Public Enterprises) I witnessed the Public Sector Enterprises' (PSEs) culture from inside and outside. I superannuated as CMD of one of the prominent PSEs. Unfortunately the post-superannuation period soon became the most tortuous time when my health waned and I was hospitalized in a critical position for almost a month. It was during this long and idle period when my younger daughter suggested that I write about my life and my days in the Indian Public Sector, recount it to make some honest confessions before the public.

Hospitals are like long pauses, big grey blotches in the otherwise colourful story of life. The very sombre facade spells impending gloom. The surroundings and confinement, bare and minimalist, make one miss life's myriad colours and we start valuing it. They have a way of getting straight to the point, telling you that this pause, this sabbatical, is meant to make you take a break from life and actually stop to think about it. For a change, one tends to view life from the other end. Suddenly, what is and what will be fades in comparison to what has been. We are drawn towards one's past as it comes flashing back and reminds us of things immemorial.

I landed in hospital on account of severe blood infection that ultimately resulted in chronic kidney ailment, and stayed there for 25 long days. This gave me ample time to unwind, recall and retrospect almost 65 years of my life's journey from childhood to senior citizenship. I was prescribed dialysis twice a week (later thrice) and I abided diligently. Each session was a four-hour procedure, which also granted me a tranquil space to reflect on my past and analyse the present. Now I do not harbour any ambition to dish out a bestselling story-cum-management bible. I do not want to leave my footprints in the form of an interesting read, but I intend to write this with honesty and a fascinating mix of my life's ups and downs and the corporate culture of Public Sector Enterprises (PSEs) in India. Perhaps, this book would help you tide over your days of adversities, like I did, managing poverty at the beginning of life and most importantly, learning to balance poverty, prosperity, wealth, affluence and influence with values during the current phase of my life. Besides, it is also remarkable how 'poverty' itself cannot be a constraint; it cannot limit one's capabilities; it cannot contain one's desires and restrain one's goals and it cannot define one's purpose in life. Rather, it can be a beautiful opportunity to realize one's full potential and can be a blessing in disguise as it brings out the value of the true assets of life. I discovered that even worst of poverty and best of richness cannot be the reason for happiness—it is something else and good health is the real means to the end, i.e. happiness.

Back home after 25 days of painful hospitalization, a first-hand experience of re-birth in all senses, I resisted the urge to jump back into the madness of work and accompanying rat-race. I presently serve as Director General in SCOPE, on superannuation from GAIL where I was Chairman and Managing Director a few years back. This period of retrospection and reminiscing the past was made more meaningful as I could share all of this with my younger daughter Smriti, who works and stays in Bangalore but was with me throughout the first two weeks of my hospitalization. It was the time when I was battling for life. Later she had to leave for London for official work, but came back to New Delhi to take further care of my health and monitor me strictly. She instantly became popular among the hospital's best doctors and was nicknamed 'Memory', which is the English translation of her name 'Smriti'.Ultimately, the inspiration to write this book came from Smriti who constantly pursued me to share my experiences with others.

I had enough idle time to ponder about the past, retrospect, and pen down the 65 years of my life, particularly the 35 plus years that I spent in PSEs in India. My elder daughter, Snigdha, was also there with me throughout my hospitalization with my son-in-law Mohit (who proved his worth more than sons of today). Anxieties that accompany such trying times were reflected in Gita, my wife, which clearly mirrored the story of Indian culture and the dedication of wives towards their husbands. Unfortunately, there often lacks a reciprocity and mutual understanding in relationships in today's life.

Sincerity in worship, persistent prayers and entreaties of my wife Gita, wishing me speedy recovery, gave me paramount force to fight back for life. Best wishes from people, friends and acquaintances, for which I am extremely grateful, brought the power of Supreme to light and once again led us to deposit our trust in His miraculous powers. He is indeed the beginning and end for all of us. After the successful transplantation of the new kidney, I got a second life.

This book is not my autobiography in the literal sense of the term, neither is it meant to be a sermonic management handbook. But, it certainly weaves the story of my life in the form of this book and shares my experiences and reflections on the Corporate PSE culture as gathered in my long years in the public sector. It also highlights issues that caused perennial discomfort to me. My tryst with the corporate culture and the popular corporate decorum, goes back a long way. In writing this book, I intend to simultaneously share and discover with you, dear readers, what can the perfect, if not 'utopian', corporate world be? Does the present system invite and demand perfection, competition and excellence at its unhealthy peak? Concurrently, the life of a CEO in PSEs is fraught with superhuman claims, on efficiency, intellectual superiority, keen and sharp business acumen, well developed and perceived market instincts, all in good equal measures. How deleterious can the life of a CEO thus become? Owing to my longstanding allegiance to the Public Sector, I also am inclined to discourse upon the ideal state of a Public Sector that can set a benchmark in the world of corporate civilization. I wish to see the Public sector re-invent itself and re-emerge to work towards advanced national goals and also compete with the private sector. Hence, I will not hesitate to mention that there is an underlying perceptible agenda behind this book thus written, and that is to understand the dangerous sophistication of corporate culture. It is a culture that needs to strike a balance between a fresh, robust and healthy life-style and prominence alongside outstanding financial achievements. Let good health, right mental constitution, fitness and wholeness, besides productivity, efficiency and dedication, become important measures of one's performance.

The book is titled *Untold Story of the Indian Public Sector* with me as protagonist of the story. It has three parts: (1) Journey from Childhood to Senior Citizenship; (2) Critical views on Indian PSEs and (3) Untold Story of Public Sector Enterprises in India. My colleagues, Miss Deepshikha Michael (Economist) and Shri Anand (Private Secretary), read through the manuscript painstakingly and I hereby sincerely acknowledge their efforts. Cooperation from SCOPE employees and my friends is also greatly acknowledged.

I will appreciate if you could also share this book with your children, which would fulfil my desire of passing on the wisdom that I acquired, through trials and tribulations in life, to the younger generation. Living a life of scarcity should not/cannot be a bottleneck in their prosperity. This information will help overcome general depression prevailing among the new generation. To sum up, it gives me immense satisfaction to share my story and the untold story of PSEs in India in this book.

If you feel that this book makes for an interesting and enriching read, do write in briefly with your views on my email address: *victory0138@gmail.com.*

Dr U.D. Choubey
victory0138@gmail.com

Dated: 3rd April 2014
New Delhi

Contents

PART - I

Journey from Childhood to Senior Citizenship

First Innings

I was born almost 65 years ago in a remote small village of Baidyanathpur in the Saran District of the State of Bihar. The English calendar objectively marks my birthday as the 3rd of April, coinciding with the birthday of Shaheed Bhagat Singh, while my mother fondly recalled and associated my birthday with Ram Navami. The village of Baidyanathpur, in the state of Bihar and the family of my father had one common factor and that was poverty. My father, an orthodox Brahmin, served as school teacher in the State of West Bengal, the neighbouring state at a place known as Barakar between Dhanbad (Bihar) and Asansol (West Bengal). Among the four sons, I was the youngest and obviously fell prey to some undefined laws of large families which demand that the youngest be the natural heir to a series of hand-me-downs. Hence my meals, clothing, schooling, etc. were but second, third and even fourth-hand experiences. However, as also is the rule with large families, I, being the youngest, got a better part of admonishments and reproaches. I slowly became adept at the art of crying, for a very long time, unabated, so much so that sometimes even forgetting the reason for weeping. This continued to attract attention of all family members, but they gradually became aware of this as my hidden strategy.

I later realized that weeping in this world does not make any difference and there are far better things to do. With such an inference drawn, it made me a master of controlled emotions throughout my life and I never came out openly ever to express them. This suppression of emotions, unfortunately, became a cause of hypertension (B.P.) which

I thus developed in the latter part of my life. The realization came at a much later stage when the die was cast and diabetes followed too. The double jeopardy of blood pressure and sugar led to chronic Kidney disease (i.e. in the last phase of life). Old habits die hard; probably I will not be able to change at this age and am prepared to suffer more. But I started advising everyone to shed tears wherever and whenever it was so felt. I counselled everyone on the benefits of sharing one's sorrows and pain with close friends even if it attracted some measure of apparent artificial crocodile tears and false sympathies from few people. Anyway, I should leave the subject of tears at this stage and move on further as I surely will find better instances to talk about it later in my life particularly I realized that tears and laughter are the sine qua non of our lives even though not a solution for anything.

My father was a strict disciplinarian. The entire family was quite often a victim of his strict indoctrination/ regulations and anger during his temporary stay at the village when he came home for summer or Puja vacations. I used to pray to God for my father's early departure from the village to Barakar school. Each time during his stay, my father prioritized a few things and his financial allocation was accordingly earmarked like money for organic fertilizer, polished fine food like rice, pulses, ghee and above all curd, etc. In spite of being an orthodox Brahmin, my father had a special attraction for non-vegetarian food but limited it to mutton and fish which he named "Ved" and "Puran" as Brahminical inhibitors used to associate psychological conventions and pressures with consumption of such non-vegetarian fares. Interestingly, and rather ironically, the other five Brahmin families in Baidyanathpur were voracious eaters of non-vegetarian dishes. However, chicken was strictly prohibited as it was considered the staple meat of Islamic community. In spite of the best part that good food was cooked during my father's stay at home, all my outward pleasures were marred by an inward fear of stringent discipline and curb on my movement outside home. Therefore, I used to do a countdown to the day before my father's exit to Barakar. My happiness increased exponentially as his departure day neared; it was indeed an inverse relation between the number of days of stay and happiness, the lesser the days, the more was happiness. Probably, this was the unusual relationship between father and sons of love and fear. My mother used to bridge the distances, for consolation if not for anything else. Later in life, I realized that discipline, character, respect for age and regard for all human beings irrespective of caste, creed, sex or religion are the real virtues. Prayers bestowed even on your worst enemies will only make you stronger. Today, I attribute all these ideals, values and righteousness to my father who had endeavoured to imbue these in our minds. An authority of three languages namely Hindi, English and Sanskrit, my father always stood for a value-based life which I consider the 'real education'. Perhaps, poverty and resulting hardships inculcate values naturally and deeply in so many middle class families; eventually pave a way for developing best leadership and sound governance principles.

I, at this stage, must tell you something more about poverty in the family. I was born in a so-called agricultural family but the total land was not sufficient to meet the full year's requirement of grains. It was limited to meet only around 7 to 8 months' requirement. Rice and wheat were a part of it but a major portion was coarse grains like maize. Evening dinner used to be an 8-cm diameter chapatti (flat round bread) made of *atta* (maize flour) with of course enough seasonal vegetables grown in the captive land—which largely included pumpkin, brinjal, radish, spinach, drumstick, lady finger (okra), smooth gourd (torai), banana and the like. But in the absence of these, *gur* (jaggery) was a common supplement. Cow's milk was outsourced at the rate of 250 grams daily only when I, or anyone in the family, fell sick for at least 15 days. Interestingly, I basked in the glory of all the attention I grabbed during my illness and additionally enjoyed being served good food and milk, so much so that often I prayed earnestly to fall sick. The habit of seeking more attention from others never diminished—I never visualized "*Shohrat ki Bhookh*" (Hunger for Importance) is always bad. Today, I acknowledge the fact that too much of anything is toxic and that too much attention brings sorrow at the end. It is better to live unseen, unknown and die unlamented. In the later stages of my life, when I got the authority and highest position in one of the best corporate entities, I got used to quoting *Meraj Faizabadi*, '*Shohrat ki bhookh mujhe bahut ruswa karti hai aur shohrat mera peecha bhi nahi chhorti*'.... But, in this phase of life, after 25 days of hospitalisation (in February 2012 with the worst of Kidney ailment my desire for being the centre of attention has started decaying and has also stopped the fear of losing anything.

Courtesy, poverty, certain necessities of life were privileges for me. As such, I was often seen in a pair of half-pants (that too went missing often) and a khaki short-sleeved shirt, which continued to be my attire for months unchanged and unwashed. Daily ablutions were something not expected of me. If at all I took bath, it was at a nearby pond called *baoli*. Being naked gave me extreme discomfort, quite like the blatant nakedness shown in cinemas today. However, this unclothed state was a natural outcome of poverty and hence was taken in a healthy perspective. Brushing my teeth, again, was not something I did regularly. Though I did sometimes indulge in long, lazy hours with my *neem datun*, sitting outside my two-room house made from partly brick and mud. It calmly accommodated 7 to 8 persons of the family. Built upon the foundation of poverty-driven sincerity, it endured the earthquake of 1934. It was disastrous and I had heard horrifying tales from my grandfather about it.

Every morning, I welcomed the first sunrays at the open field near my house, carrying with me a mid-day snack of home baked chapattis and jaggery in one hand and a *lattu* (top) in the other. Lattu was my favourite game and I was the first to reach the playground to meet my friends for a game. The seeds of punctuality that germinated and grew in me can perhaps be traced to my passion for such village games and in my unbridled enthusiasm to play that I learnt the importance of being on time—but I followed it more for play and less for schooling.

The village of Baidyanathpur was a five-family Brahmin village, surrounded by small houses of the other backward classes (OBCs), as they are referred to today. However, it was a casteless coexistence of all in which the social order was relegated to the background and cohesive living became the norm and nobody at that time ever felt being a part of upper caste/community. Probably, the most common factor driving peaceful co-existence was poverty and lack of infrastructure, so much so that the nearby elevated road made of mud was known as *pakki sadak* (concrete road), though it remained flooded throughout the rainy season. For going to Chapra (the district headquarters) one had to first go about 5 kms to get a bus which in itself was an adventure. People demonstrated how a small bus could accommodate about 200 persons—partly on the seat, some standing and largely on the roof.

I had the privilege and freedom to be out of home from sunrise to sunset (except for a small duration of lunch time) and played Lattu, Kabbadi, *chikka* and sometime *ghuchi,* which was a game played with coins (one paisa one cm diameter coin equivalent to one fourth of an 'anna' and sixteen anna making a rupee). The game was to pot the pie in small hole from some distance and hit it to win the game and earn all the coins. However, this game had to be played in seclusion and away from the prying eyes of the elders as it was somehow associated with a kind of social stigma, the one which equates such playful dealings in money to gambling. I was not one of the best at this game and lost more often. However, my elder brother Shri Birendraji, four years my senior was a whiz at it and had to be roped in by me to play on my behalf, to at least win back the coins I had lost. This was because of my brother's deep love and his affection for me, which remained till the later part of his life. He was a retired professor of BIT, Mesra, and finally settled down in Ranchi where he was bedridden because of a paralytic attack. He died because of brain haemorrhage recently. He preferred to live a life of seclusion having a clean soul, honest and non-interfering behaviour with a clear and fundamental knowledge of chemistry.

Such was life up to four years of age; it was most comfortable—free from any burdens of school, dreary routine of home-work and absolute freedom to lead a nomadic lifestyle. But started the 5th year of life and I suddenly found myself in the unavoidable whirlpool of 'schooling'. I was asked to join the lower primary school, the only school in front of my house. Arming myself with one book (Manohar Pothi), one small slate and a pencil for writing, all in one modest jute bag, I marched towards my school along with another piece of jute rug for sitting. On reaching school, I was asked to sit in a line and start with 'ka', the first letter of Hindi alphabet and also my first inning of formal education. Irrespective of all the learning and education which was initiated in my life, I was to enter my most difficult phase as 'schooling' restricted my movement, my freedom and independence which shaped and sharpened my faculties. I, quite painfully, had to sit through the entire day before my class would finish and I could go back to my meanderings. The one-room roofless school had no boundaries and the logistics were threadbare. Different corners were designated for different classes, each corner belonging to Class I, II and finally Class III, while the fourth corner was reserved for the only teacher who also had the rare privilege of sitting on an elevated mud platform from where he brandished his authority and monitored all the three classes. The elevated position of the teacher showed that he is the guru and is above all. This image was entrenched in my mind forever. The method of teaching and consequently learning was that students read in a chorus that often sounded like unintelligent gab at memorizing cum learning. The ensuing noise was a testimony to this traditional method of learning where emphasis was on numerical, rather than the reasoning faculty of mathematics. By and by, just when things were a bit settled for me, my life took an abrupt turn when my eldest brother got recruited as a civil servant and was expected to join as a trainee Magistrate at Daltonganj. This was back in 1953. This was perhaps the most memorable juncture in my life and for my family as my eldest brother had outshone his peers and made his way up the professional ladder. It was a matter of immense pride and promising beginnings, which eventually led him to be recognized as one of the best IAS officers of the State Cadre.

Amidst all this euphoria, admission to standard II in the Mission school (Daltonganj) on the contrary, was a let-down for me. To begin with, I found myself in the middle of co-education which was a blow as I had never expected to play hand-in-hand with girls in the play period. I bunked such classes and hid somewhere, which ultimately led to written complaints against me by my Christian, English-speaking and affluent headmistress. Besides, I also faced difficulties in the academic arena as I had joined midway and the other children in the class were naturally smarter and ahead of me, especially in the conversation classes as my peers spoke better English. I felt left out and inferior, which summed up my difficulties. However, the day the annual result was announced, I was pleasantly surprised to find myself amongst the top three students in my class and this became news worth circulating, as this village boy had managed to out-perform his peers! This was quite unexpected. My one year's successful stint at Daltonganj came to an end as my eldest brother got transferred to another district. Interestingly, even today, this transferability is a common tenacious disease inflicted on the Civil Servants. In one swift motion I was back to square one, in the same single-teacher, roofless school, though in class III. My performance in school nosedived to the extent of my not being able to get a veritable graduation from class III. For the first time in life, I received a favour in the form of my being declared 'passed' from Class III, courtesy village teacher Shri Bageesh Choubey, who shared cordial relations with my family. Nevertheless, notwithstanding the rustic structure of the village school, I credit my entire academic life and excellence to lessons learnt at the same village school. Later in life, I was given expressions in my PG at Science College, MBA, PhD in Hydrocarbon and another PhD in Management and finally LLB from Delhi University. I am proud of my present existence and learning experiences, without any artificiality, any pretence of luxury or pedantry, in my village and my village school. I love to talk about it to my daughters, who, even though inspired, feel amused at those funny ways of schooling was in contrast to theirs in DPS-RK Puram. For me, indeed, it has been an amazing and enriching journey from a humble school in Baidyanathpur to studying in Oxford, Canada and finally Stanford. But even today, I compliment my village school for inculcating in me discipline, character and a value-driven life, which lacked in my later part of education in college or even in the best-known foreign universities where I studied.

The instinct to learn more and more persisted in me throughout my life, which I attribute to Aphar Secondary School where I was admitted in standard IV and studied up to matriculation. Aphar School was a model school in the area situated about 5 kms from the village. All the four brothers set excellent records vis-à-vis their performance in this school. The school encouraged a lot of extra-curricular activities besides academics, like a debating society, a 'pooja' society, other hobby groups and playgrounds for football and other sports, and above all a school Parliament with a Prime Minister, his Cabinet, Opposition, a President and Vice-President. This parliamentary model was based on the Indian Constitutional norms and a monthly assembly meeting with the workings of this school Parliament was often stormy, leading to free exchange of blows which is like present day disorderly sessions in the assemblies and parliament. When I was in Standard VIth, elections were held and I was unanimously elected the Vice-President of School Parliament as this post did not attract many students. However, per chance, the President was in his last year at school and upon his passing out from school (in matriculation), the Vice-President assumed the chair of President. Hence, in standard VII, I became the Supreme Constitutional Head, the post I held for five full years, not allowing Parliamentary elections during my tenure. In fact, when the PM and his Cabinet had a major fallout with the Opposition leading to lot of quarrels, infighting and a major standstill, upon the well-intentioned and confident advice of the Hindi teacher, I declared emergency as the situation posed risk to 'internal-security', which was well within the constitutional provisions. I became the de facto, de jure constitutional head, continuing for as long as I served as the President. Later in 1977, when emergency was declared in India, by then Prime Minister, I reminisced about my days as the Constitutional Head in School way back in 1961-62, when I got a taste of dictatorship, a taste which though addictive and heady, was bitter nonetheless. I admitted to my children about my growing inclination towards dictatorial ambitions at that time in my youth. However, I feel that my despotic tendencies were checked in time by souring of my relationships with most of my best friends and well-wishers, followed by jabs at physically assaulting me sometimes. I survived the sporadic violent and disturbing episodes being an outstanding student and much liked by my teachers. Today, I know exactly why dictators usually meet with an unpleasant end, like being sent in exile, and I am glad that change in my life came much before I would have suffered a similar fate!

Politics charmed me and became my forte. It came to me naturally and I increasingly became aware of, and involved in, matters of national and international politics, sharing with everyone my views and gradually forming opinions. I even managed to catch the seasoned eye of one of the oldest persons in his village, Shri Yasashvi Choubey, fondly called Baba, who encouraged me to pursue my passion for politics on a social platform with my intelligent and sharp views on national and international political topics. A news column by late Durga Das was very popular, especially with me, which I followed throughout the later periods in my life.

Soon, my trysts with political activities and interests, with less focus on academics, reached my brother and father. Consequently, they started monitoring me and nipped my ill-fated tendencies in the bud. Special supervision was afforded to my academic performance through the teachers of Aphar School. One of my teachers, my English teacher, Shri Dhanusdhar Prasad, delivered a long lecture on behalf of my eldest brother and ordered me to attend coaching in English Literature from him the very next morning, and every morning thereafter at 6:30 am sharp. This made my life particularly miserable as I was forced to get up at 5 am every morning, even on chilly winter days, and walk bare foot for 5 kms to reach the teacher's abode. The teacher was a real Literature wizard and a strict disciplinarian, quite like my father. His special love for Nesfield grammar inspired me to a great extent even though I had initial difficulties with appropriate prepositions (like put out, put in, put on, put up and so on). Nevertheless, my love and admiration for knowledge of English literature, or even Hindi and Urdu Literature is a product of a combined influence of Aphar School, my father and brother, who were great at inspiring people, a quality rare and unmatched. This is why, though we were living in a poverty-stricken family, studiousness for achieving high standards of academic performance was inculcated and nurtured. History repeated itself when I matriculated with 1st class just like my elder brothers, who had set similar records in the same school.

Aphar School was a great experience and it is impossible to narrate everything here, neither it will be of any relevance to our readers. Nevertheless, for the readers, I would like to reiterate that the nature of an education system has a direct bearing on the up-bringing of children and a balance of academics with extra-curricular activities and sports is essential to guarantee an all-round development of students.

School education ended in 1964-65 and college education commenced at Science College at Patna University from where I completed my PG in Chemistry, breaking the record of the university with a first class position. This was followed by a PhD in Hydrocarbon, MBA and LLB..

Science college at Patna was a unique experience for me, where I hobnobbed with the best students from across the State. It was a status symbol to be or to have been a student of Science College of Patna, then considered the best college in Asia. Even the faculty was exceptional, having made their mark at National and International level. But, unfortunately, politics had entered in the academic world of Science College that lead to the creation of different groups of students and teachers. Political leaders of the State always took advantage of the situation which was aggravated by Shri Mahamaya Prasad Sinha, the then Chief Minister of Bihar as leader of Samyuktha Vidhayak Dal (first coalition government) a concept largely given by Dr. Ram Manohar Lohia who also brought "gherao" which was earlier not known in day-to-day life for jeopardizing the system. Student politics, further took a bad turn during the "Sampoorna Kranti" led by Shri Jaiprakash Narayan, a genius and a generous mass leader who thought himself as an alternative best Prime Minister but was frustrated throughout his life and could not succeed. Sampoorna Kranti influenced prominent leaders from Bihar like Shri Laloo Prasad Yadav, Sushil Modi, Ram Vilas Paswan and Nitish Kumar. Outcome of group politics had a bad effect in the State. Certain important events are worth quoting here, which had a bearing on my life. For the first time in life, I witnessed how the faculty granted favours to their favourite students. Their favours were either based on caste, community lines or other such considerations. Loyalty and sycophancy was rewarded by such obvious special treatment. This disturbed me to a great extent and I sought for answers to such discriminatory practices in politics. Perhaps, this was the event that triggered an active interest in politics in me. I was attracted towards the leftist forum and this gave me an opportunity to meet some national leaders like Hiren Mukherjee, Jyoti Basu, A. K. Gopalan, Sunil Mukherjee, A. K. Sen, and soon all of them recognized me by face. Marxist forum was not the end of diversion in my life. It transgressed further in active politics. Some of the best students of the time had become very active and even undertook underground activities to voice their opinions. Some of them have stuck with this lifestyle and still must be in hideout. Class annihilation was their philosophy. I would have become an outlaw and a hard-core Naxalite (1968-69), but for a bombing instance at Patna College. Some four to five students died at that bombing and I called it quits. Later, I realized that this was the right decision as most of the activities of Naxalites became tainted with crime, owing to misguided and misdirected approach towards their goals. Vested interests overshadowed the interests of the class-less and caste-less society. For me, this brought an end to my inclination towards Naxal philosophy.

I was never a serious student and was never wanted to study till late night. Each day by 9 pm, I retired to bed and started my mornings by scanning all the morning newspapers, sharing the news with my eldest brother when he returned from a morning walk. My eldest brother has remained a role model for my entire life and continues to inspire me. We commuted to college by a bus where a very interesting duo, Badri and Sahdeo, the bus driver and conductor, made the short journey to and from college an enlivening trip. Badri's job was to take out the silencer of the bus as soon as the bus started in order to make maximum noise. This came in handy when following and generally overriding a girls' bus off and on. Among the seniors commuting in the bus was Laloo Prasad Yadav, who was fair, smart and slim in contrast with the rough and blunt appearance he wears today. He was the student's Union President. Probably the basic nature of a human being remains the same throughout his life even if there are changes in his/her physical appearance, the former bestowed by the Almighty and the latter artificially bred by the person.

For me, poverty was still a prominent part of my daily life as I got 30 paisa every day for the to and fro student bus ticket. That was all I had when I left for college in the morning at 9 am till I returned at 5 pm to finish my day's waiting leftover lunch. Nonetheless, my mission was to perform well and today I have a high regard for my days of scarcity and struggle. Poverty highlighted another aspect, one which was a blessing in disguise. I, like most of my friends, did not roam about with girlfriends and don't remember to have ever proposed any girl decently or indecently. Romance was not my forte and I astutely checked any such advances from the girls' side. Above all, I do not have any regret for the same.

Happiness visited again when I topped the list of students who successfully passed in M.Sc. Chemistry. This came as a surprise, not only to my family, but even to my faculty, my friends and students of the academic year. On the day the result was announced, I was accompanied by my brother to the University, where the results were put up on the notice board. As soon as we reached the campus, my brother and I were surrounded with students congratulating me for unexpectedly topping the University examination. This excited my already anxious brother, while I dispelled any such news as a mere rumour as I recounted how I often joked in class with fellow students that any attempt by any student to excel at examinations was futile as I would undoubtedly top the results. The joke, however, became reality and I returned home with my brother to celebrate one of the happiest days of my life.

So the first phase of my life came to an end with the completion of the PG course. Obviously the next step was to search for a job, ushering me into the 2nd inning.

*****

Second Innings

Childhood, school days and even college education in my life established a firm belief that scarcity can never be a constraint, rather it builds the character of an individual on the foundation of love, patience, respect and real value based education, all brought by the inspiration and blessings of the parents. For my brothers and me, our father laid down this foundation with strict discipline and prevented common vices to invade and influence our individualities. How often I look back and recollect his fatherly counsels. My brothers and I achieved the best in our respective lives, be it Civil Service, Doctor or Academician and today I, highly qualified, and a CEO of Navratna, now Maharatna PSE.

I was at my father's bedside when he breathed his last at the age of around 78. I feel my father's absence greatly when today I could have given him all the comfort and luxuries of life. For a person well versed in three languages, English, Hindi and Sanskrit, and a deep knowledge of Literature, my father was entitled to a better life. My inclination to literature can be traced to my father's mastery of the same. Merely listening to my father chanting Sanskrit *shlokas* during the morning prayers was a treat and I learnt all of these *shlokas* by heart which I still remember. The passion and respect for languages made my father insist on my learning Urdu Literature from a Muslim *Qazi*, a long bearded Mullah. The idea did not go down well with me as I considered it belittling for a Brahmin boy (7 years in age) to study from a Muslim Qazi. With my narrow-mindedness and egotism I refused to attend any such tuition from a Muslim Qazi and I made my situation clear to my father. My father had only two things to say; first, 'The Muslim Qazi was a teacher to me and a teacher is equivalent to God, hence I should treat my Muslim teacher with utmost respect and reverence. Second, one must, absolutely have respect for age in life and consequently, I should value my teacher irrespective of the religion.' This however did not deter me from my decision and I discontinued with his Urdu classes from the third day itself. Little did I know that twenty years later, my love for Urdu language and this incident would haunt me and eventually compel me to make one last desperate attempt at learning Urdu, the beautiful and pure language and its charming poetry through *Khat Kitabat Urdu Course* conducted by Jamia Millia Islamia. The effort, though futile, made my attachment with the language only grow over the years and I even dabbled in Urdu poetry, penning down some beautiful verses myself. This blunder, as I call it, made me realize the importance of valuing teachers and elders, qualities I solely attributed to my father. I learnt over the years to understand how human relationships, leadership and finally success depend on how one deals with people. Every individual, big or small, sitting in front of you is your ambassador of goodwill and treating them well with respect works wonders. With this learning, a legacy from my parents, I began the second phase of my life and slowly stepped into the Indian PSE Corporate World.

Searching Job

The immediate requirement was a job. Incidentally, the job market was very poor and even an outstanding academic performance could not secure a decent job for me. The entire socio-economic affairs of the state of Bihar were in complete disarray, marked by complete apathy of the government and social system towards such decadence of the economy. Rampant corruption, bureaucratic red-tapism, officialism by people in power, etc., had eroded the work culture, making the state economy lose control. The 'Sampurna Kranti' call given by Jaiprakash Narayan was totally misdirected, especially among the youth who twisted the very contours of this great indigenous ideology and mixed it up; crime and hooliganism became routine for them! Undoubtedly, a genius and a visionary, Jaiprakash Narayan was a leader of the masses. His ability to reach out to the people and speak in their language was reminiscent of none other than Mahatma Gandhi. However, somewhere down the line in his political career, his philosophy and ideas got caught up in the politics of unfulfilled desires to be a powerful leader, mirroring frustration and to certain extent desperation. The unfortunate fallout of this was the uncertainty of the methods with which this ideology was asserted, advanced and dismissed. Even the academics suffered. Students suffered as the sessions in colleges and Universities got delayed by up to two years! This led to a lot of problems relating to the credibility of students from Bihar and they were considered only as a last choice in the job market. For me, this was a frustrating period, when even with an exceptional record of academic performance, I could not land into a good job. A brilliant achievement (in 1971) followed by a long wait till the 1st quarter of 1973 for a permanent job was highly frustrating. Though I got an offer to teach in the capacity of a temporary position in a degree college at Patna, which was a unique experience in itself as most of the students in this college boasted proudly of having criminal backgrounds. They came with a vermilion sign (*tikka*) to college to proclaim their standing and superiority. I was apprised of the criminal environment of the college by the other staff members who admitted that all of them had been abused and even beaten by these students on some pretext or the other. Fortunately, I escaped this sordid reality as the students went on an indefinite strike and out of the 10 months that I was to serve, I had to attend college for two months only. The examinations were a farce as neither the teachers nor the students took them seriously. Unfair means of copying and cheating were rampant during the examinations.

Life in Bihar was difficult as it had lost its glory. All hopes in the state had been shattered and there was no sign of any hope for the future. The political leadership was busy making their ends meet and made massive amount of money at the cost of plundering the economy of the state. Bureaucracy became more political than development-oriented and the state that was bestowed with rich mineral resources became the poorest state. People enjoyed free ride and marauding activities were uncontrolled. *Dadagiri* became the way of life and the most lucrative entrepreneurship as law and order was in the hands of the people instead of being a government agenda. Youth suffered the most. Poor parents from villages who sent their children for studies were in an insecure position. "Sampoorna Kranti" furthered their plight except for the fact that some of the youth leaders were born out of the "Sampoorna Kranti" in a direct benefit for them otherwise it would have become a "Sampoorna" flop. People forgot the revolution under "Sampoorna Kranti" soon and it finally died with the death of Shri Jai Prakash Narayan.

One day, while I was still serving as a teacher in the college, an excise inspector came to meet me. He had come to fetch me for a meeting with the Excise Commissioner (a senior IAS officer of State) and took me to his office in Secretariat at Patna. We rode in a government jeep and this made me feel very important and much in demand. However, this feeling of pride was short lived as the inspector on the way to the secretariat, explained as to what the job profile of a chemical examiner demanded from me. The job required the examiner's signatures to accord for approval of sale of food, beverages, fruits and other such edibles in the state. Each approval had a lot of hidden money behind it which would be taken care of by the inspector, entailing hardly any effort from me. The inspector chattered away about how good his previous boss was and how his boss had managed to make three to four palatial houses in a very posh area of the state capital besides purchasing acres of land!

I understood quickly as to what was being conveyed by the impudent inspector. Upon meeting the Commissioner, the first question I asked was when I would be able to become a Class I officer as the existing post was in Class II. The Commissioner was quite taken aback as he had never been asked a question like this before. He told me very clearly that his predecessors had throughout been very happy and content with their Class II positions, on which they joined and retired. It was difficult situation and I asked for a week's time to think about the offer. I never got back to the Commissioner and I preferred to lose the opportunity to build palatial bungalows! In a similar situation in 1986 I resigned from a senior position in Food Corporation of India (FCI) within five days of joining. Making easy money was not my cup of tea.

Initial Days of Entering the Corporate India

But every dog has his day, and one day, after a year of struggling in search of a job, I got the first permanent offer in the then P&D, (now PDIL at Sindri then in Bihar, now in Jharkhand), a consulting organization in fertilizer and chemical under the Central Government. PDIL was a prestigious Central Public Sector Enterprise; it was a status symbol during the time. It had a beautiful township at Sindri. Working in an Industrial Township had benefits but not away from few notable disadvantages. A major benefit was in thc form of united efforts they could rely on to tackle their common personal problems. Negative fallout of such a close-knit society sometimes sets off the feelings of envy that people harboured against each other. Any personal incident would easily spread by gossipmongers to the detriment of the person concerned. For entertainment, there were very few avenues, one of them was a small club with limited seating capacity (in fact limited standing capacity too!), which screened movies on weekends and attracted large crowds. The club served as a platform for social get-togethers more than entertainment.

The decay of PDIL had started in the 1970s and it coincided with my joining in 1973. That was my first experience of the Corporate world. Unfortunately, it was a dissatisfying experience where employees had freedom to go to office at any time, at their convenience, and often remained without an actual job. I was really frustrated by the work culture in the 1st PSE that I joined.

Thirteen years (1973-86) of life at PDIL were nevertheless eventful. There was the enthusiasm of a first job, and mission to do something better in life combined with quick frustration as PDIL was in a decaying stage and employees gradually preferred to live in a comfort zone. A laidback attitude was widespread. Soon they became habituated to do nothing that lead to a bad corporate culture. It was a matter of shame to see a zero-level initiative in an organization that was highly reputed. Its reputation gradually diminished as compared to other public sector organizations. Earlier, the integrated part of the then Fertilizer Corporation of India (FCI) was reduced in status, once FCI was brought into pieces and PDIL was given separate independent corporates. PDIL became a rather non-entity immediately after new gas based plants at Aonla, Guna, Jagdishpur, Bhatinda and Shahjehanpur were commissioned during the latter part of the 80s. For me, it was a difficult phase and I finally reached a conclusion that I must leave the organization quickly. The organization gradually became almost extinct because of its own huge manpower of 3600, but thanks to economic liberalization and freedom to face open challenges, it was revived by a cut down on the huge manpower to 510. Today, it is heartening that it is a profit-making organization.

I was determined to leave PDIL and I got offers simultaneously in April 1986 from Food Corporation of India (FCI) and the other from Gas Authority of India (GAIL). On the advice of my elder brother (an IAS officer in Bihar), I joined as Zonal Manager in FCI at Lucknow on 22nd April 1986 and was placed as incharge of Vigilance Division. Heading Vigilance Department in Food Corporation was a unique experience indeed! It was a great opportunity to earn enough money to bring all the luxuries in my life, but for the fact that within a week of joining, I decided to quit FCI and resigned, which became a news in FCI. FCI had an altogether different culture and a new experience too for me and I realized that either I was not fit for the job in FCI or the job was not fit for me. A week's work experience in FCI enhanced my frustration as compared to PDIL. As Zonal General Manager of Vigilance in FCI Lucknow I knew a lot about corruption in offices. Nobody could be found above board and the culture in office was all for making money, building real estates and boldly facing vigilance administration. Within three days of joining I assessed that the world of FCI was not my cup of tea and before the end of that week, I left for the headquarters of FCI at Delhi to submit my resignation. Of course, before submitting the resignation I went to GAIL (at Samrat Hotel) and met Shri R.P. Sharma, who was heading the Marketing Department, and informed him about the entire episode. I also requested a one-month extension, as the maximum allowed period granted was over. Shri Sharma talked to Shri Kapadia (the Director In-charge) and I was granted another one-month extension to join. I submitted my resignation at FCI, and in my case the minimum period of one-month notice was waived. I joined GAIL on 29th April 1986, the same day that I was released from FCI. I had chosen to refuse the opportunity to amass wealth and luxuries. This was the story of losing another opportunity to amass wealth and luxury of life – the dream shattered!

At GAIL

I remained a loyal employee in GAIL till my superannuation in 2009. I had joined as Sr. Dy. Manager (Marketing) in 1986 and gradually reached the highest position as Chairman and Managing Director in 2006. It is difficult to tell the entire story but some of them are eventful that I am sharing here, as they can't escape the memory horizon, and the same will tell a lot of what is happening in the corporate culture--a great learning experience on joining GAIL. My boss was Shri R.P. Sharma who headed the Marketing Department. I learnt many qualities from Shri Sharma and that served as one of the most important factors to reach the top of the ladder.

I am forever grateful to Shri Sharma for his guidance, both academic enrichment as well as Management Control. There may have been times that I might not agree with some things, but irrespective of all, I acknowledge Shri Sharma for being the stepping stone in the early stages of my corporate sector.

Like the usual natural process, among the CMDs of GAIL, all of them had different qualities. Shri Vineet Nayar, who had earlier left IAS to join GAIL en route to World Bank was an excellent visionary and laid a foundation for GAIL and its dynamic expansion programme. His vision to have a petrochemical plant at PATA (Auraiya) in Uttar Pradesh became a good source of revenue later for GAIL. He had a very good influence on bureaucracy because of his past association. A number of LPG plants were conceived and finally commissioned during his time, which increased the bottom-line of GAIL. Later, LPG transportation by pipeline became assets for GAIL. GAIL was also allowed the marketing right of LPG in retail marketing but lost the right because of intensive campaign against it by an oil marketing company. Shri Vineet Nayar became a role model for me when I became CMD (2006-09). GAIL was lucky to get authorization for five long-distance pipelines to increase the transportation of natural gas up to consumer's premises. These pipelines became lifeline for GAIL in the future and are branded today as my big achievement as CMD.

GAIL Delhi had a different culture altogether. It was a miniature of what is prevailing in other public sector. Commissioning of HBJ pipeline was the prime concern of GAIL. First, gas supply was started with IFFCO Aonla and NFL Guna and Indo-Gulf Fertilizer Jagdishpur followed quickly. But suddenly it was realized that it became suboptimal utilization of the pipeline as remaining/designated gas-based fertilizers were far behind commissioning even though the capital-intensive HBJ pipeline had been commissioned. Again, it was the vision of Shri Vineet Nayar that Marketing Department was asked to survey small/medium consumers in and around Delhi. About 22 new consumers were added after great effort as it was difficult to convince them about utilization of natural gas. Every day officers/staff were in the field for joint meetings with prospective consumers. The year 1987 was a difficult time for the marketing department. But, soon industry became addicted to natural gas as their economics became highly attractive besides better quality of finished products.

It was beginning of an organizational rivalry between ONGC and GAIL when the entire retail gas transportation and related assets of ONGC were transferred to GAIL in 1992. As most of the managers in the beginning came from ONGC to GAIL, it started inducing ONGC culture. But for the better influence on bureaucracy, GAIL gradually became known for its own brand and culture. I had been identified as the tough crusader to take the right of transportation of entire gas related assets from ONGC. Alas it has gone back to ONGC now, to some extent.

Successor of Shri Vineet Nayar, namely K.K. Kapoor and C.R. Prasad, lacked the vision of Shri Nayar but pursued the policy/projects for their successful implementation. Shri C.R. Prasad was an excellent Project Manager and his art of monitoring the project was admirable and worth learning. Then came Shri Prashanto Banerjee from outside (IOC) to take charge as CMD in GAIL. His autocratic way of controlling the employees totally demotivated them and many young engineers left GAIL. Attrition rate increased and there was an atmosphere of loss of faith among the employees. Each one became suspicious of the other. Charge-sheeting became the way of life. The organization moved towards disintegration. Administrative Ministry was completely axial to Shri Banerjee and wanted to get rid of him at the first instance. He was humiliated on most of the occasions in the Ministry. He was denied extension of term even though he had over a year left to reach the age of superannuation. I was Director (Marketing) and for most of the issues I was called by Ministry to know anything and everything related to various issues ongoing in the organization. Shri Banerjee had a habit of writing long letters to Ministry which was disapproved by all level of officers in the Ministry. But all blames cannot be attributed to Shri Banerjee. Civil servants not only in India but elsewhere too carry a common liability of ego. Probably this must have been the realization when Edmund Burke wrote that "if you allow Civil Servants to rule, people will welcome for first few months but after that you will find all Civil Servants hanging at the nearest lamp tower". In case of Shri Banerjee ego-driven pseudo supremacy led ultimately to his removal from the post of CMD. I was one of few who disliked the way he was removed.

I as GM Marketing also faced similar situation. As Marketing Head, everything moved around me as all information/clarifications sought by the Ministry or anywhere came to me. Unexpectedly, I was transferred to Kolkata where there was no gas related work with no transmission line or customer. It was a good period to take it easy and I utilized the time for writing my first book on natural gas and at the same time acknowledged the authorities for the unexpected transfer to Kolkata. There was reaction in the organization as many similar, important and arbitrary transfers took place earlier as well. The organization was in turmoil and the atmosphere in the organization had become suffocating. The organization started losing its credibility and no new project was assigned; qualified engineers and MBAs started leaving GAIL. For me circumstances and events suddenly changed and I was promoted to Executive Director and brought back to Delhi, placed in the Noida Office, ironically in GAILTEL, a small segment of the telecom sector. In Kolkata, I got a call from Shri Banerjee to congratulate me with a sarcastic remark that my promotion and placement is like the deity of Puri where "hands of the God has been cut-half". I understood that I had been removed from his main function (Marketing), but I never represented this time also. Destiny was moving somewhere else for me, to an unexpected position. Within six months, I was selected as first Director (Marketing) and within the next two years as CMD of GAIL. Naturally, both the positions I assumed did not come without opposition. As Shri Banerjee was not given extension of CMD's tenure, I had become eligible for the position. Ultimately, the existing scenario provided the opportunity for me to become CMD of GAIL for 30 months. I became the CMD when GAIL was going through the most difficult period.

I became incharge of a highly demotivated lot of employees, working in a culture of no initiative, crest-fallen, no projects in hand, discarded relations from the administrative Ministry—and all this came as big challenges. The day I joined I went to the Ministry and requested for five new pipelines to be constructed by GAIL in phases. To my surprise, I got the go ahead for all the five pipelines which was the turning point in the history of GAIL. Implementation was done on priority. I realized that without motivation of engineers, managers, staff, it will not be possible. The first thing I did was to bridge the gap between different layers of personnel for information dissemination. A lot of monetary and non-monetary incentives were given and it took one year to bring the employees back on the work track. The entire prevailing extravaganza was cut back and measures were taken for spending frugally. To inspire everyone further, a statue of Mahatma Gandhi was installed in the lobby. Simplicity and prudence probably became the biggest strengths for me in GAIL.

It was an innovative way that I as CMD presented before the Board my agenda of thirty months (the tenure) and gave commitment to complete activities of different directorates, which finally became Board approved KPA for Directors incharge. All directors gave their maximum output to fulfil the required responsibility under KPA. Each month's meetings were held to review the "CMD's agenda". I must confess that in spite of best efforts it was difficult to get support of all directors. This comes naturally in a hierarchy that people on other ranks often throw challenges in the smooth working of an organization, not realizing that such attitudes weaken the organization. Sometimes, the concerned Director is exposed, dislodged and demoted for one reason or the other. He carries a bad impression inside and outside even after he leaves the organization.

For me, GAIL was the real test of corporate culture. I learnt to survive under adverse situations. I also learnt that I had to manage the world on my own and nobody was going to rescue me from challenges. I had to absorb all the shocks in the day-to-day workings and counter the adversaries, competitors, etc. The cumulative effect of various stresses built up being a CMD and led to serious health problems that generally come when one superannuates. It happened with me too. I superannuated in 2009 with hypertension and diabetes, which finally became the cause of damage of both the kidneys and hospitalization for 25 days, and eventually a transplantation of kidney.

Realization came much while I was in the hospital. At the same time, it gave enough time to think deeply and revisit the past of almost 37 years in public sector where I started from the first step of the ladder to reach the highest position of CMD. It was a marathon journey with so many ups and downs in my career.

I received appreciation from all corners and superannuated from GAIL with massive goodwill from employees and others in oil and gas sector. It was wonderful to see that all the officers of oil and gas sector, especially who were always adverse to each other, had transformed, became approachable and helped each other. They had willingly adopted my initiative of the mantra of "3C", i.e. Cooperation, Collaboration and Competition. Public Sector in India has neither been perfect in the past nor will be in the future because bringing change in public sector is a Herculean task. All efforts could make little impact unless attitudes change. As I had totally impregnated into the public sector mind, I continued to put substantial efforts to bring change in the otherwise inertia-driven culture. I never gave way and continued my efforts like during the 25-day hospitalization I shared all these happenings with my younger daughter Smriti, who inspired to me write my memories so that others could take good lesson to protect their health. I, therefore, did not write with an intention that this will become a best seller, but definitely expected to draw satisfaction from this as I will be able to write honestly and share the untold story of Public Sector culture in India. Lastly, besides the story of the Public Sector and so many realities in life, including my life in public sector, I thought it will help guide the top management to shape their future in better ways.

Altogether, I spent a substantial 23 years in GAIL, it would not be possible to describe all the events as it will defeat the objective of telling the untold story of PSE. But some of the events could not escape from the memory line. Also such events will reflect the prevailing culture in PSE.

With dialysis thrice a week and life support largely dependent on medicine and external support, I wrote the story hastily in order to complete it. You never know life and I did not want to leave it unfinished in case my health deteriorated.

Now the four years out of the 5-year term were over, and I was approaching senior citizenship. The chapters that follow describe the stark and harsh realities and may be offensive. It was essential to conclude the book with suggestive ways and means for protection of the health and future happenings of chief executives of public sector organizations and also bring the much-needed change in the so-called "Temples of Modern India" and "the Commanding Heights". Today, the fact remains that these "Temples of India" are being sold out in parts to meet the budget deficits. The holy cow has become milking cow now in spite of the fact that PSEs in India have shown exemplary performance; they have come to be good means to better budgetary support to Government.

I had two unexpected transfers in GAIL—one to Baroda (in 1992) and the other to Kolkata. Both came as surprises to me and everybody in GAIL. My transfer to Kolkata was rather irrelevant as there was no gas transaction in the pipeline of GAIL in the entire West Bengal. But Shri Banerjee after joining GAIL as CMD had a pre-conceived opinion about me that could also be a misconception, because all activities moved around me as General Manager - Marketing. This was probably because of a very long period of association with marketing functions.

The Kolkata transfer was as if to shift me out from mainstream. My response to Shri Banerjee when I was asked to go to Kolkata was interesting in action because I immediately asked my PS to book a ticket for Kolkata so that I could join the very next day. It was an anti-climax for Shri Banerjee who probably could not resist asking why I was so enthusiastic to join the work in Kolkata. I responded saying that Kolkata would be a great place as there would be enough idle time to write a book, which I was keenly planning since long. In fact, there was no work for me in Kolkata. The reply was obviously not liked by the CMD. Irrespective of anything I liked Kolkata as I completed my first book and above all I got the opportunity to worship in all the temples of West Bengal, Guwahati and Tripura including Ganga Sagar. In fact, I complemented the top management for this punitive posting in the acknowledgement of my first book transparently.

During my interview, Shri T.K.A. Nair, the then Chairman (PESB), browsed through my CV for the post of Director (Marketing) and asked, "You have been a marketing man—how come you are being placed in the Telecom Deptt."? I still justified my placement by saying that it was my CMD's confidence in me because GAILTEL required a strong marketing man. It was a highly sarcastic remark when he said that "he had read the acknowledgement part of the book". It wasn't my intention to embarrass the other observers and interviewers present there. I was finally selected and occupied the front room opposite to the CMD's on the sixth floor of GAIL Corporate office. But that was not the end. Within two years, the post of CMD was circulated and I applied as this was my last chance to apply because of age eligibility. Selection of CMD in PSEs is nothing less than the selection of a Secretary General of UNO, in fact, even more difficult. My selection as CMD was probably unique as I could gather that it was against the wishes of then Secretary (Petroleum). Some delay in processing was obvious but finally I got ACC appointment in February, (thanks to Shri Suresh Pachauri, then DoPT Minister in-charge) and joined immediately. I faced opposition openly after being selected. Ironically, many congratulatory messages came my way from CEOs present in the programme of National Petroleum Sports Body Awards ceremony. I spoke in one line that I am the government nominee and will deliver better than earlier CMDs. Later, there were a number of occasions when I was snubbed.

Equity Sale of ADB in PLL

When I opposed the same and requested through a long letter to allow four partners and if not by them to GAIL (India) Limited for purchase of equity of ADB in Petronet LNG Ltd.

The second such occasion came when 10% equity dilution of Oil India Ltd. was to be offloaded to the oil/gas sector. An agenda for Cabinet had been prepared to allow 2.5% each to BPCL and HPCL and balance 5% to IOC. I met the then Minister Petroleum Shri Murli Deoraji, who readily agreed and asked me to inform Secretary, Petroleum, Shri M.S. Srinivasan to prepare a Supplementary agenda as the Cabinet meeting was scheduled the same evening. I never expected that Secretary will practically tell me to leave the room but like a daredevil I told him I as CMD was employee of the Secretary as owner and therefore it is giving much needed relief as the issue has been registered in Secretary's mind. It was total frustration for me.

I superannuated in 2009 as a satisfied CMD. That ended my service in a PSE but destiny made me Director General of SCOPE which is an Apex Body to Pursue Excellence in PSEs—altogether 260 in number and the same gave me opportunity to know the corporate culture prevailing in PSEs. But the thirty-month period was bound to have ups and downs for me. On 31st July 2009, I called it a day in GAIL and proceeded to start my professional life's last inning at SCOPE Complex.

Last Innings

On superannuation from GAIL (India) Ltd. in 2009, I joined as Director General in SCOPE (Standing Conference of Public Enterprises). SCOPE was a small family of around 60-70 employees and about 300 contract workers for maintaining the two huge buildings known as SCOPE Complex on Lodi Road and SCOPE Minar at Laxmi Nagar. Each tower accommodated about 40 offices of Public Sector Undertakings. Entire maintenance was done by SCOPE with contract labourers. Obviously the usual problem of Contract labour and litigation was the liability of the SCOPE Secretariat. Director General (DG), SCOPE, was the head of the Secretariat. It is a totally DG-driven organization with of course an elected Chairman, Vice-Chairman and 19 Executive Board members. Elected body is ceremonial only but sometimes the Chairman of SCOPE overexerts depending upon his nature and relation with DG. I continued good relations with successive chairpersons.

On joining SCOPE as DG for a fixed period of 5 years, I found that it was more challenging than GAIL. You must be wondering how SCOPE was more challenging than GAIL. Honestly, there was no systematic approach to any issue in SCOPE. Probably the successive management considered SCOPE a good platform for merry-making, entertaining officials and as a means to some good end like sympathy of Ministry, foreign visits and personal visibility. It was a true representative of Public Sector culture.

My joining as DG coincided with a breaking point in life with so many past and present mental pressures—I could either quit and join a number of lucrative offers from the Private Sector or continue on easy-going life as DG, SCOPE. But both options were against my nature. Private Sector as concentration of capital in private hand was not fit for a country like India for at least hundred years. Private ownership of capital brings further gap between rich and poor in a country where human development index hovered around 1.4 for the last thirty years. Obviously, the choice was limited to SCOPE. It was the third time that I chose to reject the chance to earn wealth. (Two times earlier I rejected offers in Excise and then in Food Corporation of India, mentioned earlier in this book).

SCOPE comprised largely of people from the older generation who lacked knowledge of modern principles of management and governance in the ever changing world. It was more challenging to change their mind set. They had spent a quarter of the century living in a comfort zone. Unfortunately, complacency had set in and they had no desire to expand their horizons. Much of this had to do with the culture in SCOPE. With the proposed changes, all of them were anxious, though gradually their mind set started changing. It is rightly said that old habits die-hard.

All the employees, irrespective of their position and Central pay scales, were accustomed to work like labourers. They never applied their mind and were neither permitted to do so for bringing in excellence in the prevailing system.

Within a week of joining, I categorically told each one to either change their mind set or they will be forced to change it mandatorily. It wasn't their fault alone; the other side of the coin was equally to blame. SCOPE being a small set-up, continued to operate as it required with no focus on the fact that there were employees who were so dispirited and unacquainted with the current needs, few were simply sycophants and above all it was male-dominated organisation. They worked on small budget as establishment cost, which came from subscriptions from a little over 200 public sector constituents and some surplus generated from important programmes/participation. In a way it was self-sustained and the best part being that Government aid was not accepted and neither was donation from private-owners taken. Probably they knew that any aid taken from Government would hinder the way the organisation worked and ultimately result in being an extended arm of the government.

The liability of a bunch of demotivated employees before me was the biggest challenge. SCOPE was better identified by the two towers, one at Lodi Road and the other at Laxmi Nagar. The activities were not known rightly so as there was no activity worth mentioning. I understood that SCOPE must have an identity as a body that pursues excellence and professionalization in public sector management. Accordingly, I introduced an International Leadership Development Programme, which was conducted for one week in India and for two weeks in Europe. Similarly, the programme on Corporate Governance was modified to include training to Independent Directors, which is an essential part of a Board managed company in India. These aspects will be taken up later in the days to come in this book. Further, in order to give identity to Indian PSEs, 10th April was earmarked for "Public Sector Day" every year which was generally observed, coinciding with Public Sector Awards given by the President of India. A Public Sector Flag was also launched and unfurled by the President of India on 10th April. These two initiatives gave the much needed identity and publicity to the organization.

The unfortunate part in SCOPE and probably the reason for its non-identity and its redundancy was the demotivated employees, even though they always completed the ad-hoc requirements of the Chairman, DG and the Board efficiently and with a family-type approach. They lacked initiatives and a change in their aptitude and attitude was needed. They worked like robots when asked to on ad-hoc basis. It is shameful for both employees and their controller to reduce the workforce to such a level and probably the controllers/ employers are more to blame as compared to employees. One of the fundamentals and the mandate provided to SCOPE was to bring in better leadership quality, enhanced management tools and assimilations with the changing world order, but SCOPE Secretariat could not change, neither could it change the PSE culture. I saw negativity as a significant factor in SCOPE and in many large PSEs and I will highlight it further in the book.

SCOPE employees had compromised with their fate that nothing is going to change with respect to their career and future prospects, and welfare. The work output was only according to the diktats of the superiors. I considered in my heart to either quit or take up the challenge more vigorously. I opted for the latter even though I suffered with a severe chronic kidney ailment that required transplantation. I was undergoing three days of dialysis in a week for four to five hours in each day and also working, which became a tough task, but I continued. Firstly, I could not continue to stay without work, and secondly, I naturally required money to sustain myself in the future. It became very difficult to consider a kidney transplant outside India because I had no money that was required to meet the cost of transplantation. Ultimately, there was no way other than selling the ornaments of my wife and daughters to mobilize money along with savings made so far. Public sectors have medical coverage for superannuated employees but it does not include medical expenses outside the country—be it for a life-saving treatment. I requested for a Board approved policy even though it might not cover my case as being the past case. Personally, I feel that life-saving should be given due importance more than anything and meeting expenses in such cases deserves national consideration. I prefer to leave this issue at this stage.

One of the chronic problems in SCOPE was a large number of Contract Labour who under a court order got salary without doing the job for which they were initially taken in. This problem is like a legacy that exists not only in SCOPE but throughout the country, largely due to ill-treatment of labour force. SCOPE, in particular, was carrying this huge liability for long time. I gradually started settling the issues one by one to the satisfaction of both contract labourers and the PSE constituents. The same demotivated SCOPE employees worked hard to reach to an amicable solution and they deserved to be complimented. There was no incentive for encouraging such work therefore, I initiated it gradually. A reform was also initiated for career growth and this resulted in a change in the employees' outlook. It was a great day for SCOPE employees when they suddenly found that a Social Security Allowance was announced for superannuated employees. Today, SCOPE is a changed organization and I am confident that given proper motivation, they will continue to perform better.

A study by Ernst and Young to articulate vision, mission and restructuring of SCOPE has been initiated. Maximum emphasis has been made to bring larger visibility and promote brand image of SCOPE to reflect a non-commercial, transparent and action-oriented body that plays a neutral role for bringing professional excellence in PSEs. As change is not always welcomed and so was the case in SCOPE. It was very difficult to change the attitudes of the employees of SCOPE who are largely older and demotivated people. They had no motivation to utilise their strengths and give a good output. I had joined SCOPE considering that my job will be lighter but on the contrary there were a lot of time-consuming tasks as compared to what I had done as CMD of Navratna company in my earlier active period. I diagnosed the basic problems with the employees and I have no hesitation in saying that motivation and lack of incentives combined were responsible for this state of affair. While the employees considered office as a place where they idled time away, the elected members and even the Government department were also not concerned. The understanding was mutual. I realized that a change in the prevalent atmosphere is needed necessarily to tackle such attitude, which would bring a large change. Obviously this called for more physical and mental stress for me. SCOPE Secretariat was accustomed to work under pressure for various programmes. Every pressure was exerted typically till the time the study was awarded but nobody cared for the outcome of the study. It appeared that once the order was placed and part payment was made, all the interest taken earlier came to zero. It was very difficult to attract focused attention of PSEs whose priorities were different.

I introduced a few innovative ways to bring SCOPE in the limelight. As mentioned earlier, 10th April became the Public Sector Day all over India and presentation of SCOPE Meritorious Awards and SCOPE Excellence Awards enhanced the prestige of SCOPE with the President of India or the Prime Minister of India gracing the occasion. Seeing better visibility of the Public sector, private industry chambers also started trying to rope in public sector in their obvious interest. A Public sector flag was launched by the President of India.

Almost after six decades of existence of PSEs, SCOPE has witnessed significant changes from time to time in PSE culture. In the pre-1991 phase, PSEs were a tool to employ many unqualified people that led to an impression that PSEs, even though branded as "temples of India" became inefficient and a liability. However, with a change in the post-liberalization period PSEs showed exemplary performance. Today, PSEs are largely self-sustained and do not ask for any budgetary support. It is a fact that few financially stressed companies have to necessarily depend upon Government support. Time has come when there is a need for a drastic review of policy with respect to revival of these companies. These financially stressed companies are being run by demotivated employees or the Board who are considered as failure as compared to other profit-making companies. The fact remains that these sick enterprises never changed with time for which both government and the enterprise are equally responsible. SCOPE provided various opportunities for me to know of the corporate PSE culture, and 260 PSEs have a different story to tell. Some of the stories are untold so far.

A Rough Ride to Senior Citizenship

I never knew that reaching the stage of Senior Citizen would be the most difficult period for me – a rough ride altogether. The double jeopardy of diabetes and hypertension during my days at GAIL and subsequently in SCOPE had drained me, so much so that both my kidneys had gone weak and finally damaged in 2012. Unfortunately, in the life of a CEO there is hardly any time to pay attention to health. The stress and strain give rise to a number of unforeseen troubles for them and when they realize the importance of health, it is usually too late. The die is cast. It so happened to me.

About four years after my superannuation from GAIL, suddenly one day (25.2.2012) I found that my legs were swollen, followed by vomiting and breathing problem, which forced me to see Dr. Chopra (Cardiologist) in Moolchand Hospital. On initial examination, he found that the pumping rate of the heart had come down to merely 13% against the normal 60%, which could result in a cardiac arrest any time. Immediately he admitted me to Intensive Care Unit (ICU) and informed my wife to call my near and dear ones as the situation was critical. I was not told this but knew that about 20 litre of excess water had flooded in my chest/lung and abdomen which resulted into breathing problem. It took three days for Dr. Chopra to tell my wife that the critical time was over, but both my kidneys had been damaged to the extent of more than 95%. I stayed in the hospital for about a month fighting for life. They advised me to immediately go in for dialysis and subsequently plan to get a transplant done for a new kidney from some donor. They immediately created a fistula, connecting an artery and a vein in the left hand after a minor surgery. Dialysis was done twice a week, initially for four hours each day extending finally for three days a week for five hours. Even then I preferred to attend office in SCOPE either before or after the dialysis. This book is a good consequence of the days that I was suffering and struggling for life—an outcome which is for better or for worse.

After a little over one year of dialysis, doctors asked me to go in immediately for a transplant failing which could lead to multi-organ failure. As I was the youngest among the brothers (three of them are no more) and none of the parents were alive, I had no way than to search for a potential donor outside the family. Kolkata is one such place where there is a possibility to get potential donors. My initial efforts for three months were futile and disappointing because of greedy donors and middlemen. I lost all hopes for survival, but suddenly, one day a thirty-five-year-old young boy appeared before me and offered one of his kidneys. As I had bad experiences with earlier potential donors, I asked him about his preparedness to go to Singapore to which he agreed. Accordingly, I reached Singapore in mid-May (2013) and I was examined by Dr. Lye of Mount Elizabeth Hospital. After completing all other formalities, I was admitted in the Hospital on 17th June. Successful transplantation was done by Dr. Tan on 18th June. I was sent to ICU again and except for initial hick ups, I was released after 12 days. It was tortuous and highly painful experience to be in the hospital, as a matter of fact even after release. Complete physical chemistry changed. I was unable to walk, speak or sleep—far away from a normal life. But all said and done, it was second life for me. Things remained painful even after four to five months but then they gradually improved.

It was a realization that came late that CEOs have to give importance to their health first to be able to handle themselves and the organization smoothly. They are subject to tortuous stress and strain for obvious reasons. It is ultimately health which will be the cause of happiness, particularly in the latter part of their lives. Working for achievement of objectives and goals in public sector without any due/undue influence will not only enhance the performance but also result into better health of CEOs. I had to suffer the worst period of my life before I could reach the stage of senior citizenship. I want to conclude that the road to senior citizenship was not easy. But then, struggle is a fact of life.

PART – II

Critical Views on the Indian PSEs

Public Sector - A Milking Cow

I feel privileged with almost 40 years of association with the PSEs (1973-2009)—36 years directly and the balance years in SCOPE (Apex Body for Public Enterprises). It has provided me with the privilege of having an insight into the prevailing state of affairs in the Public Sector of India. I experienced many ups and downs and witnessed the disturbing side of corporate governance. Some of the critical views on prevailing practices in Public Enterprises in India are shared ahead.

Public Sector in India have played a crucial role in the economic growth and social transformation of the country for over six decades. It has emerged as an institution of strength and prowess and the prime vehicle that set off the entire post-independence industrialization process and infrastructural development. Entrusted with the task of facilitating nation building, the sector has come a long way extending its scope of operations to realize economies of scale and fulfilling the agenda of inclusive growth.

Six decades of public sector has been the history of development and growth. The first phase, i.e. post-independence and pre-liberalization period has been the era where social objectives were important than commercial benefits and profits. At that time, Indian economy was ridden with extreme disparities in income, wealth and consumption. The locus standii of public sector was socio-economic development. Soon after independence in 1947, it was realized that the country lacked infrastructure and industries. There was a complete crunch of financial resource even though there was large and cheap labour force. The economy was rather based on agro-sector. Realizing the need, five PSEs with an investment of Rs 29 crore were set up at the time of the First Five Year Plan. During the period, Public Sector recruited about 24 lakh people which resulted in over-staffing, besides a number of decisions were taken to provide social justice to the people of the country. As a result, public sector witnessed huge losses and was branded as inefficient and a drain on national resources. Profit was considered as dirty word. Therefore, Public Sector became a symbol of inefficiency where productivity was a casualty.

In the post-liberalization period, the sector entered the new era. After the first phase of development focusing on creating vital infrastructure of the economy, it was triggered by the launch of the New Economic Reforms in early 1990s. Displaying resilience in countering the challenges of the new era, the public sector performed admirably well, and emerged as a major force.

Over the years, PSEs witnessed phenomenal growth in terms of investment, production as well as in scope of activities. Today, there are as many as 260 PSEs with a total investment of Rs. 7.29 lakh crore as on March 31, 2012, and return on investment is over 18%. Through its consistent performance and robust contribution public sector has sustained the growth of Indian economy. It provided the much needed cushion to the government and the economy during the economic meltdown. It not only sustained its growth momentum but also anchored the Indian economy against severe jolt to its growth. This can be seen from the fact that during the period of global economic recession, i.e. 2008-09 and 2009-10, the public sector registered positive growth of 3.7% while world over there was negative growth of the corporates. In terms of wealth generation, there are enough statistics to substantiate their contribution to the economy. In the year 2011-12, CPSEs posted net profit of over Rs 97,000 crores and contributed over Rs 1,60,000 crores by way of duties, taxes and dividends to the central exchequer. The turnover as percentage of GDP contribution was 22.1% in the same year. It is also pertinent to mention that since the introduction of disinvestment policy in 1991-92, the government realized over Rs. 1,13,000 crores from the disinvestment process as on January 2012. They have also been playing a crucial role in earning precious foreign exchange which is of the order of Rs.1,25,000 crore in 2011-12. Pursuant to its role in overall economic development of the country in the last five years in the post-recession period, the investment of public sector has been more than 3 lakh crore. Interestingly, increase in investment is being increasingly financed from PSEs' internal resource generation which is indicative of the continuing expansion of the sector and indicative of the fact that PSEs have constantly reduced their dependence on government's budgetary support which is little over 2% presently. The above are only indicative of the proof that the public sector is playing its role of being an 'engine of growth' for the economy truly well in the emerging economic scenario.

The growth story of CPSEs without highlighting the social upliftment undertaken by them as in the contemporary environment, commitment to the financial bottom-line is no longer the only appropriate focus for a company, an equal focus has to be on what is known as 'triple bottom-line', i.e. People, Planet and Profit. Accordingly corporate is not viewed as an instrument to serve interest of its shareholders but also of all its stakeholders including society and people at large. Moreover in a country like India where there is extreme social and economic disparity, the need for CSR should be the prime concern. PSEs since inception have an unparalleled record of contributing and shouldering the social responsibility and integrating their business strategies with sustainable initiatives. With the aim to bring about radical transformation in the quality of life of the under privileged, PSEs have gone a long way in achieving their goals and translating their policies into deliverables through positive intervention in social upliftment programmes. It is a matter of pride that their CSR strategies are aligned to national priorities to meet the basic needs of citizens like literacy enhancement, educational aids, providing drinking water, community development and infrastructure, environment protection, health care and family welfare, etc. They have been earmarking about 2%of their net profit for carrying out CSR programmes much before the enactment of new Companies Act which has a mandatory provision of CSR for all corporates. Public Sector in India adopted CSR responsibilities not only in letter but spirit also because CSR is not a wastage of money but rather an investment with good return, branding and in line with objectives set for PSEs. As of now, there are 260 PSEs categorized as Maharatna, Navratna, Miniratna, Non-Ratna and financially stressed companies. The list can be seen as *Appendix – I.*

The importance that the public sector attaches to the society at large can also be seen from the fact that out of total CSR contribution of INR 1,765 lakh crores by top 100 Indian companies (based on net sales of 2011-12), more than 40% contribution is by 37 public sector companies alone. PSEs have been actively contributing to the socio-economic developmental objective of the government. Economically, they are making active contribution to the central exchequer by way of taxes, dividend pay-outs, interest payment and foreign exchange and on the social front, their coordinated efforts has led to employment generation, skill development, infrastructure development and helping the government in distraught times by way of contributing to PM and CM Relief Funds. There cannot be two opinions about the fact that PSEs have been instrumental in effective implementation of national policies of the government aiming at balanced and equitable development across the nation.

Corporate Governance in PSEs

Governance is the key issue today. It is derived from the Latin word "Gubernare", which means to steer or to govern. Originally, the term Governance denoted exercise of power and acceptance of accountability thereof in the running of kingdoms, regions and towns. In the current scenario, it has become a major issue and essential requirement for socio-economic development and overall inclusive growth. Accountability is the key to good governance today and has expanded beyond the basic definition of "being called to account for one's actions". Accountability and Corporate Governance are sine-qua-non with each other. Over the years, these two have found significant relevance in the corporate world. Two main drivers which have led to an integration of Accountability and Governance with Corporations are: increasing incidents of unethical practices and debacles which took place in corporate domain in the recent past. The rat race for reflecting higher growth, inflated profit generally through accounting systems, and concealed liabilities gave rise to a large number of frauds in the corporate world.

The forces of deregulation, institutionalization, globalization and tax reforms have made the minority shareholder more aware and vigilant. This has necessitated the companies to adopt practices that entail them to go beyond legal compliances and adhere to standards which are not only ethical but also make businesses socially more relevant. In earlier times ownership of the Company was not widespread. Modern day companies have, however, become increasingly dependent on external resources for meeting their needs which has led to widened ownership and brought about a need to segregate ownership and control. This has also necessitated that the management of the companies be responsible to their owners, i.e. shareholders leading to development of the concept of Corporate Governance. From "No One's Agenda" Corporate Governance became "Everyone's Agenda". As a result new institutional mechanisms, such as codes, best practices and standards have initiated fresh thinking at the boards as well as at the level of strategy formulation and its execution. Moreover, with corporations expanding their businesses in multiple jurisdictions, compliance management has assumed international dimensions as well. Corporate laws, intellectual property laws, labour laws, tax laws, securities laws and various other laws affecting corporations required a structured approach for unflinching compliance. These notable developments made corporates to reposition their thinking to enhance shareholders value and sustainable competitiveness. The transformation and transition of corporate attitude and way of functioning to good governance was most desired for the PSEs (PSEs) as they embodied not only profit making but also socio-economic development of the country and were accountable to the people at large.

PSEs' significant role in accelerating the pace of development in the country has been facilitated by sound, prudent and transparent business principles and practices. They are guardians or trustees of precious public money. They deal with tax payers' money and have to uphold values to achieve goals and objectives for which they have been established. Under such circumstances there is a need for set of rules/code of conduct to guide the actions and conduct of these enterprises.

Corporate Governance in PSEs is more robust than in most private counterparts. Numerous checks and balances have been introduced to secure high level of accountability. They are kept under effective Parliamentary controls. Accountability of CPSEs to Parliament has been ensured through various mechanisms which have evolved over the years. Questions on wide range of issues and facts are raised through Parliament Questions and CPSEs are mandated to give absolutely correct and complete replies. The Parliamentary control of CPSEs is also exercised through the elaborate set of committees including Committee on Public Undertakings (COPU), Consultative Committee of the Administrative Ministry, Standing Committee of Parliament for administrative Ministry and their sub-committees viz. Estimates Committee, Committee on Government Assurances, Rajbhasha Committee and SC/ST Committee. In addition, the Annual Reports of CPSEs are also tabled in the Parliament. Apart from the Parliament, PSEs are also accountable to other authorities like Comptroller and Auditor General (CAG), Central Vigilance Commission (CVC), Competition Commission of India (CCI) and Right to Information Act (RTI), etc. Further, the CVC has asked all PSEs to consider signing the Integrity Pact Agreement with Transparency International's India Office that would help them ensure transparency, equity and competitiveness in procurement and contracting processes. Many CPSEs have already signed this Pact that contains rights and obligations to the effect that neither side will pay, offer and demand or accept bribes; collude with competitors to obtain the contract; or engage in such abuses while carrying out the contract. RTI is applicable to Public Sector on the pretext that they are based on public money (Tax payer's money). The only regret is that there should be level playing field by bringing all the enterprises on the principle of equity because of the fact that each enterprise stands on Tax payers' money only. The entire money is public money except it is black money.

Guidelines on Corporate Governance are issued by Department of Public Enterprises for Central Public Sector Enterprises (which are applicable to listed as well as un-listed CPSEs) and cover issues such as Composition of Boards, Audit Committees, Subsidiary Companies, Remuneration Committees, Disclosures, Code of Conduct and Ethics, Risk Management and Compliance. It has also been mandated in the Guidelines that there should be a separate section on Corporate Governance in the Annual Report of all companies with details of compliance.

These mechanisms and systems have certainly created and sustained the confidence of people at large in the CPSEs. It is widely acknowledged that PSEs are open and transparent ensuring fairness in their transactions within and outside the company with investors, customers, employees, partners, competitors and society at large. Still the governance part is at low level in India and has not been able to bring confidence of investors as witnessed in developed countries viz. US,

UK, France, Singapore, Norway, even Vietnam, China, New Zealand, Sweden, etc. For example, more than 42% of personal saving is invested in equity of enterprises in United States whereas in India it is less than 1%.

Corporate Governance Issues in PSEs

Traditionally, PSEs are more prone to compliance and conformance as compared to performance. This is because of excessive control of Government through administrative ministry so much so that PSE Boards have been reduced to the status of extended arm of administrative ministries. While PSEs have been following regulations, it has been occasionally realized that excessive regulations bring a state of over-governance which tilts the playing field against PSEs. Therefore, it is important that law and regulation should be updated to reflect changing responsibility of the Board in order to safeguard them in raising the corporate standards. Moreover, many existing systems and procedures are incompatible with the efficient and successful operation of PSEs in an increasingly competitive economy that is moving towards deregulations. In these times PSEs need more enablers to achieve performance levels comparable to their competitors in the private sectors as well as MNCs coming to India. In this regard, we must learn from changes being brought in developed and even developing countries as mentioned in subsequent pages.

Some of the key issues faced by the PSEs are as below:-

Multiple and Unclear Objectives

The performance of any commercial enterprise is closely linked to the objectives set for it. In case of PSEs there happen to be a multitude of stated and unstated objectives, emanating from various quarters, which are often not in conformity with each other. In fact, there is no clarity on the objectives under explicit ownership policy and that of Board policy. The result is a diffused set of goals without a proper performance evaluation mechanism. Absence of clear-cut objectives under ownership policy that is vague, complex and even contradictory and leaves scope for passive ownership and excessive interference on the Board of enterprises because of extraneous considerations.

Special features of ownership policy are:

- The owner must be clear about the objective of the policy for deciding fundamental outcomes
- Appointment of Board Members
- Appointment of CEO and Succession Planning
- Remuneration
- Investment
- Projects
- Mergers and Acquisitions
- Arrange Capital
- Dividend Policy
- Social Contribution
- Environmental Protection
- Must be deliberated widely with Stakeholders including Minority Shareholders
- Specific with Constitutional and Regulatory Norms
- Specific Target, Operational and Financial Profit, Debt Ratio, Dividend Policy, Social Contribution
- Selection of Board Members/Independent Directors
- Constraints in Evaluation of Accountability of the Owner
- Documentation for wide circulation/disclosure
- Disclosed to all Stakeholders and Evaluation against Benchmarked Policy against the objective by Independent Expert Consultant of repute

We are far away from such a clear and distinct ownership policy. In the absence of clear ownership policy for Board, investment choices made by them are sub-optimal, resources tend to be allocated to non-core activities, and it becomes difficult to mobilize resources and act freely without any interference formally or informally.

Functional Autonomy

Autonomy in PSEs is one of the key issues for the effective functioning of PSEs and much has been talked about it on number of Forums. While Maharatna, Navratna, and Miniratna schemes have granted enhanced autonomy to PSEs, it appears that real objective has not been served yet. Even today PSEs are considered as an extended arm of the government. To elaborate, the CPSEs face the problem of excessive political interference in their day-to-day operations of the enterprise. Where at one end the PSEs are encouraged to compete with the private companies, it is a distressing fact that these enterprises are shackled in many ways alien to a free enterprise. The irony of the situation is that PSEs are every now and then treated as the 'personal fiefdom' of the ministries. This is evident from the fact that the Prime Minister in 2004 issued letters to his cabinet ministers instructing the ministers not to treat the PSEs as their 'fiefdom' or 'profligate' in order to adhere to good corporate governance practices. It would not be unwise to say that the public sector has become 'milking cows' for the government. The right phrase for the public sector in India would be 'hapless milking cows'. The recent developments make it evident that the Government has categorically asked the cash-rich PSEs to either invest the surplus in a time-bound manner or deposit it with the Government as special dividend. Such persistent demand for special dividend or cash surplus is coming in wake of the need to check increasing fiscal deficit of the government since the target of disinvestment is far from being achieved. A mounting fiscal deficit is likely to reduce the international investment outlook for India and also falsify the commitment made by the Finance Minister at the International Monetary Fund meeting in Washington recently, wherein the Government assured that fiscal deficit would be contained at 4.8% of GDP. This is in addition to the fact that earlier this year the cash-rich CPSEs were at the receiving end of the government for bailing it out of the rising fiscal deficit which the government had planned to meet through disinvestment of certain public sector companies. The capex utilization of PSEs is on hold in absence of clearance of projects because of several reasons including environment and forest clearance, land allocation and similar extraneous factors. Sharp fall in rupee against dollar and unfavourable investment market in India led to a shortfall in disinvestment target. In such a scenario, the government contemplated and even directed certain PSEs (such as Coal India Limited) to buy-back their own shares using the available cash surplus with the PSE so as to reduce its fiscal deficit and meet the disinvestment target. This move of the government has not found favour as the process of buy-back is likely to impact the 'cash' position of the CPSEs under various administrative ministries. Also, a decision on the buyback arrangement of many CPSEs is pending on account of paucity of time and delay in approval by the respective administrative ministries.

There is lack of clarity with respect to how the surplus is to be invested by the government or CPSE. The government is in the process of developing guidelines for utilization of such surplus funds to boost investment and growth (by self or CPSEs) though the process of devising guidelines by the government has still not crystallized despite of the government issuing stern instructions to the PSEs in 2012 to either use the surplus for capex or give it to the government. This was indicated by Finance Minister during a meeting organized by SCOPE between the Prime Minister and heads of 25 CPSEs. During the meeting, heads of various CPSEs had voiced their inability to take decisions on investment of cash surplus on account of multilateral checks, regulatory clearances, lack of autonomy, etc., and assurance was given by the government that the issues would be looked into. Besides following the monetary liberty of the PSEs, the government is also plaguing them with constant political interference resulting in lack of operational autonomy thereby shackling them in many ways. This situation is worsened by differences between administrative Ministry and the Board. The fact that the PSEs are forced to carry political agenda to an extreme leads to loss of considerable time in implementing even elementary decisions. This is evident from the fact that it took decades for even nationalized banks to computerize their operations due to fear of mass retrenchment. It can be seen from the fact that India's largest bank, i.e. State Bank of India, began computerization only in 2002. Also, many PSEs run on the mandate of development of backward areas adding to the losses which drains out the resources of the profitable PSEs. Therefore, there must be a compromise in economic and social consideration so that PSEs could compete on global basis. To add to the socialist agenda and operational handicap is the lack of financial autonomy. Their decision making with respect to use of finances is crippled by the administrative ministries by necessitating formulation of 'a business case' for fund raising and seeking approvals for making investments leading to inordinate delays. Despite over two decades of liberalization, the government continues to view the PSEs as a means of clearing its own fiscal follies.

Separation of Ownership and Management of PSEs

Accountability in public sector structure has three parts. One is the *Ownership function of the State*, second is *Board* and third is *Executive Management below the Board level*. Let us first examine the accountability with respect to owner.

There is no denying the fact that a lot of empowerment has been announced by the Government under the Maharatna, Navratna and Miniratna PSEs, however, there is still a need of complete separation of ownership (of the Government and Board level management of PSEs). The tendency to get involved in actual management of PSEs needs to be resisted by the government. Even today respective administrative ministry officials have their own ways to influence and command the CEOs through various procedures like Appointment of Chairman and Members of the Board of Directors, decision on major policy matters such as Investment, dividend declaration, Wage Policy, Pricing Policy, etc. At the same time CEOs do not exercise the power given to them without knocking at the door of the Ministry. Therefore, there should be balance between autonomy and state control where ownership should not transgress into the managerial domain. Functional autonomy is essential for good performance and suitable guidelines must exist for the areas where the Board must seek prior government approval and where it may take a decision on its own. A policy of selective government intervention in the management of PSEs will deliver effective results. It will not only lead to increase in productivity but will also help PSEs to become globally competitive. The existing level of delegation of financial and operational autonomy to Maharatna and Navratna PSEs may be considered to be enhanced in terms of:

- Maharatna and Navratna companies should be fully empowered to decide merger/acquisitions/JVCs.
- Empower Boards to approve foreign travel plan of CMDs.
- Empower Boards to determine the compensation package of its employees.
- Periodical review of financial powers of Maharatna, Navratna and Miniratna in light of domestic and global economic environment.

Professionalization of Board

With regard to accountability of the Board, the corporate world, of late, has witnessed continued pressure for professionalization of Boards to reflect better performance. It has been observed that expectations of all the stakeholders, particularly people at large, have been mounting thereby necessitating Boards to move towards excellence and professionalization. PSEs Board represents a complex coalition of diverse and heterogeneous partners namely Functional Directors, Government Nominee Directors and Independent Directors. Functional Directors are full-time directors who are promoted generally from within the talent pool below the board level and possess strong functional capabilities and domain expertise. However, they may be deficient in strategic perspective as their transition to the board is a major paradigm shift in their vision and responsibilities. They lack interconnectedness of their domain knowledge with vision and strategy. This necessitates good scope of training in the process before joining the functional Board.

Government Nominee Directors are appointed on the Board by respective administrative ministry and are generally people of high intellect. Owing to their position of privilege, they exercise a degree of formal and informal influence on the Boards of public enterprises, which in turn, may be influenced by several considerations, including political and social requirements of the government. It is a matter of great concern that Government nominees for Directors maintain a gap with Board members and management executives which is a big bottleneck in providing better corporate governance by the enterprise.

The third constituent of the PSE Boards are the Independent Directors who are expected to exercise oversight on the functioning of the Board based on the best practices of governance and ethical standards. They are supposed to have an independent opinion and be a watchdog for adherence to best practices on corporate governance and act as conscience keeper during the Board Meeting to provide unbiased judgments. Moreover, Independent Directors are not elected or nominated without interference of the Ministry. The present way of their selection indicates that they are rather "dependable Independent Directors". Additionally, they are deficient with respect to operations and working of the PSE.

The benchmark position with respect to Corporate Governance is corporate behaviour, vision, strategy formulation, strategy implementation and strategy monitoring. In addition, Integrity, Fairness, and Ethical Behaviour of the Board Members are very important for better governance. Governance is best when we have delighted customers, satisfied suppliers, willing investors, motivated employees, happy creditors, assured and confident government, protected environment and uplifted society and community. Better governance convergence of all the above three pillars/constituents is imperative for an efficient and effective working of the Board. This can be achieved through continuous and effective training programs wherein a platform is provided to each type of director (i.e. Functional Director, Government Nominee Director and Independent Director) to understand their role and responsibility on the Board towards the PSE and the stakeholders. Through these training programs efforts should be made to identify problematic areas and identify possible solutions around them so that they can be implemented by the respective directors.

Towards fulfilling this objective, steps have already been taken by SCOPE under the aegis of DPE wherein a number of director training programs are organized in the form of conclaves and seminars, however, a lot more needs to be done to fill the gap.

Professionalization of Boards cannot be achieved unless the Board members are made accountable through a structured performance evaluation mechanism. Evaluation of Board with respect to individual members against benchmarked key performance area done through expert outside consultant should be done with right to recall Board members wherever required. There must be a mechanism to guard the guardians.

At this juncture another point that merits consideration is with respect to pre-condition of remaining term of service for appointment at a Board level position. Presently, a person is eligible for board level appointment only if there are at least two years of service left prior to superannuation in case of same company and three years in outside. In such a scenario, it has been observed that at the time when board level positions are vacant, highly deserving and competent people are not promoted to such positions on account of marginal shortfall in tenure condition. This results in de-motivation of such employees which reflects in their present performance. This practice should be improvised and consideration should be given to deserving employees even if they fall short of the required condition.

Succession Planning

The competence and ability of the Board in discharging its duties depends upon making the right selection keeping in mind the experience and expertise needed in specific areas. However, the present system is not so effective in selection of top management posts. Additionally, many Board level positions are lying vacant in PSEs and a number of PSEs are headless. Time taken to process the ACC appointments is also very long as appointment of CMDs and Directors are overloaded and quite cumbersome. Each proposal undergoes several stages, passes through a number of departments and multiple agencies. Furthermore in each stage, the movement slows down and gets delayed because of various reasons which may be further lengthened once the vested interest factor surfaces. Under such a situation an interim arrangement is made till the final selection. This leads to loss of efficiency, productivity and hampers future business perspective and strategy.

The relevance of Public Enterprises Selection Board cannot be undermined. However, at the same time, there is need to maintain its credentials as an impartial and independent body. To lessen political and ministerial influence, and ensure selection of appropriate person for top management posts, there is a need to reform the process of selection of Directors and CEOs through a robust transparent system so that notification of the selected candidate is made on the same day when they are selected. This will save good time during the period of transition when PSEs are run by a temporary acting-CEO before the permanent incumbent takes over. Additionally, PESB should be given more power as competent independent Authority so that the efficiency of public sector increases to high level.

Appointment Procedure of Independent Directors

As seen above, institution of Independent Directors is a corner stone of Corporate Governance. Such directors are appointed primarily for their contribution towards company's strategy and bringing objectivity in policy making in an independent manner. They act as a harbinger for striking balance between individuals, economy and social interest. Given the recent backdrop of global economic turmoil, and widespread corporate scandals/frauds, expectations from Independent Directors have risen considerably. They play a critical role in promoting transparency and accountability in the board decision making process. This is particularly true for PSEs where the Government is a major stakeholder. However, delay in the process of appointment of Independent Directors has posed enormous problems in PSEs and there is an urgent need to make it speedier and simplified. This is evident from the fact that at present, there are approximately 200 vacant positions for Independent Directors in various PSEs.

Further, as of 2012, 25 CPSEs did not have independent directors due to non-initiation of proposals for appointment of such directors by their respective administrative ministry. Inordinate delay in appointment of Independent Directors leads to non-compliance of CG norms which may have deleterious consequences on corporate governance reforms in India. Hence, the appointment of Independent Directors should be done in a time-bound manner, i.e. before the term of the existing independent director expires. It is also pertinent to mention that developed countries have initiated selection through a separate, independent and impartial Committee eliminating the role of administrative ministry to escape undue interference in the selection of independent Directors. Administrative Ministry's nominees on the Board are gradually being eliminated.

Creation of Additional Posts

Boards require more strengthening and better professionalization in view of high order of financial involvement and quick decisions for implementing projects. At present, Maharatna vests the respective CPSE Board to create below board level posts up to E9 level, to wind up all below board level posts and to make all appointments effect internal transfers and re-designation of all below board level posts. However, it cannot be denied that delegation of additional powers upon Maharatna Company means, delegation of additional responsibility and accountability which needs to be effectively exercised by senior and competent professionals. Therefore, need has been felt for creation of E-10 level posts who would supplement and accelerate the efforts of the Board in exercising these powers professionally and facilitating top Management to concentrate on strategic issues. Similarly, powers of other profit-making companies should also be enhanced with respect to creation of below board level posts.

Pricing Policy

'Pricing', which is one of the main drivers of competitiveness and market share, is not controlled by the CPSEs on account of socio-economic considerations such as impact on the poor, which takes priority over cost and profitability. This can be seen from the plight of ONGC, OIL and GAIL, who are mandatorily required to take the burden of subsidy for under-recovery of Oil Marketing Companies.

Audit and Vigilance Issues in PSEs

The core issues concerning Corporate Governance are also related to audit and vigilance.

As far as audit is concerned, the Comptroller and Auditor General (CAG) has a dominant role to play. The basic purpose of audit is to aid the management in adding value to the organization by providing the stakeholders and the management the benefits of an independent evaluation. Audit should enable PSE managers to develop a new culture of taking speedy complex business decisions without diluting accountability. The vigilance plays an important role. However, empowerment and enabling of the Public Enterprises is necessary for them to meet today's challenges so that they become capable to take bona fide risks and take quick decisions with the confidence that will be judged by overall results rather than by their failure in certain decisions. Unfortunately, today, the Public Enterprises find themselves in a cultural paradigm where there is premium on not taking decisions instead of on taking decisions. The fear psychosis related to vigilance function is leading to risk aversion in PSEs thereby inhibiting their performance. To streamline the vigilance administration in PSEs, CVO of the company should be from public sector background who has wide exposure and experience of PSE functioning. Further, no anonymous and pseudonymous complaint should be taken up for investigation by the CVC. Also, for board level appointments, once the vigilance clearance has been forwarded, no further complaints should be entertained.

Right to Information Act, 2005

PSEs come under the purview of Right to Information Act, 2005 (RTI Act) while the same does not apply to private sector. There should be a level playing field for the PSEs vis-à-vis their counterparts in the private sector. The vital information shared may be wrongly capitalized by competitors that can lead to exploitation of PSEs and its business goals. The subject of RTI shall be taken up later in this book.

Conclusion

In the present era of globalization, 'state-owned enterprises' or 'public sector enterprises' are not just bound to stay but also shine as they are in an advantageous position of seizing better opportunities. This not only positively impacts the enterprise but also advances the nation's strategic interests. Though the linkages of the PSEs with the economy as a whole are more complex, this should not be hindrance in making such enterprises more competitive against their private counterparts. The beginning has already been made with limited autonomous powers given to the 'Ratna' Enterprises. However, the need of the hour is to unshackle them and withdraw from the present 'close supervision of the government' form of running so as to enable the enterprise to swim on its own. Probably this was the consideration that the first Prime Minister, Pt. Jawaharlal Nehru, while debating in Parliament in 1956 on Five Year Plan spoke of:

"*.....The way a government functions is not exactly the way that business houses and enterprises normally function. A government rightly has all kinds of checks, as it deals with public money. Usually, it has time to apply these checks. But when one deals with a plant and an enterprise where quick decisions are* *necessary, which may make a difference between success and failure, the way a government functions is not sometimes suitable. I have no doubt that the normal governmental procedure applied to a public enterprise of this kind will lead to the failure of that public enterprise. Therefore, we have to evolve a system for working public enterprises where on the one hand, there are adequate checks and protections, and on the other, enough freedom for that enterprise to work quickly and without delay."*

(Jawaharlal Nehru,
May 1956, Debate on 2nd FYP in the Parliament)

International Trend

The post-recession period witnessed remarkable changes in worldwide trend in Corporate Governance. Failure of free-market forces brought a shift in the mind set of policy holders towards ownership policy where consideration moved from private capitalism to State capitalism. It has been realized that State as major equity holder has better option for economic stability and welfare of State. Latest trend worldwide portrays relinquishing of the ownership control of the Administrative Ministry and creation of the Sovereign Wealth Fund to enable State to acquire higher equity in domestic and international market. Interference of the Administrative Ministry has also been a concern in many developed countries including Sweden, Norway, U.K., France, China, Philippines and even Malaysia. Some of the developed countries have created Independent Sovereign Committee, away from the control of Administrative Ministry that monitors the implementation part, succession planning including selection of Independent Director. The practice of Government Nominee Director is also being gradually done away with. State Owned Assets Supervision and Administration Council (SASAC), China; State Capital Investment Corporation, Vietnam and Khazanah in Malaysia are notable examples of managing the State Owned Enterprises.

In India, there is need to review the Corporate Governance norms in line with the worldwide trends. Appointment of yet another Expert Committee like that of Kumaramangalam Birla, Narayanamurthy, Naresh Chandra and JJ Irani is the need of the hour to further enhance the Corporate Governance reforms in India.

DEPENDABLE INDEPENDENT DIRECTORS

Independent Directors on Public Sector Boards are highly intellectual people, but they have not contributed to the extent required. They are selected by Minister in charge of administrative Ministries and the selection process is such that they become "dependent", rather than being "independent" on the Board. The time has come for review and radical change in the selection process of independent Directors through an independent impartial nomination Committee without the influence of administrative Ministry and Minister in charge. There is also a need for recall if they do not perform their duties and responsibilities which could be evaluated by an outside expert consultant of repute. This is needed urgently when we talk of bringing excellence in Corporate Governance.

Need for good and effective corporate governance has been gaining momentum over time. Although the concepts of corporate governance have emerged in developed countries like US and UK, they have been transplanted to other countries in the last decade, including India. The phenomenon of transplantation in India can be ascribed to various reasons primarily being globalization. With liberalization, international events were having a rippling effect on India. Opening of economies and privatization resulted in influx of foreign investments necessitating 'own' corporate governance norms in light of failure of the ones crystallized by the developed economies. In addition, post-liberalization era may be viewed as a time where 'governance' encountered 'rude shocks' with increasing growth leading to the need to reflect higher or inflated profits through accounting systems such as concealment of liabilities resulting in financial frauds. With this, corporate governance became 'hot currency of the day', from being 'no man's agenda' to 'everyone's agenda'.

Securities Exchange Board of India ('SEBI') was established as the Indian securities market regulator. With economic liberalization, a major turnaround was also being faced by the Indian PSEs as a result of which in 1997, the Department of Public Enterprises (DPE) introduced 'Navratna status' for CPSEs meeting the laid down criteria. This 'status' included autonomy in decision making in various spheres subject to fulfilling of certain conditions which also included restructuring of Boards to include at least four non-official or independent directors. Therefore, it can be said that CPSEs were the pioneers to the concept of 'independent directors' in India. Subsequently, National Task Force was formed by CII in 1998 wherein a code for 'desirable corporate governance' was recommended which was voluntarily adopted by a few companies. Understanding the need for a formal framework for 'corporate governance', a committee under the leadership of Kumarmanglam Birla in 1999 was formed which led to establishment of a legal framework for corporate governance in the year 2000 in the form of Clause 49 of the listing agreement wherein the concept of 'independent directors' was also introduced. Post the infamous 'Enron Scandal', SEBI instituted Narayana Murthy Committee so as to bring about significant changes in Clause 49 in light of international developments and lessons. Correspondingly, Ministry of Corporate Affairs instituted the Naresh Chandra Committee in 2002 and J J Irani Committee in 2004-05 to examine various issues pertaining to corporate governance and Companies Act, 1956. The Narayana Murthy Committee brought about significant changes in the concept and institution of independent directors and the revised Clause 49 (in its present form) was introduced by SEBI in

2006. The Naresh Chandra Committee also recommended on various areas surrounding independent directors including definition, independent directors in audit committee and training of such directors. Most recently, DPE has issued guidelines on corporate governance for CPSEs which was patterned on Clause 49 of the listing agreement and aimed at improving board practices and other elements of corporate governance in CPSEs (including non-listed CPSEs). These guidelines were introduced in 2007 and are voluntary in nature.

Present Legal Status of Independent Directors

An autonomous board of director in companies is seen as an integral element of any country's governance norms. The fact that independent directors have taken a pivotal status in corporate governance has increasingly pinned hope as well as responsibility on such directors. The legal framework of corporate governance in India has also identified the need of independent directors and hence, provision with respect to the same has been integrally incorporated in the framework.

Companies are governed by two basic legislations in India:

- Companies Act, 2013 (replacing erstwhile Companies Act, 1956)
- Clause 49 of the listing agreement issued by SEBI

While the Companies Act is applicable to all companies (listed or not), Clause 49 is applicable only to companies listed on recognized stock exchanges in India.

Clause 49 of the Listing Agreement

Clause 49 of the Listing Agreement outlines in detail the compliance to be undertaken by every listed company in India. As per the said clause, where the Chairman of the board is a non-executive director, minimum 1/3rd of the Board shall constitute of independent directors and where the Chairman of the board is an executive, minimum 50% shall constitute of independent directors.

Further, the Clause defines independent director as a non-executive director who:

"*...apart from receiving director's remuneration, does not have any material pecuniary relationships or transactions with the company, its promoters, its directors, its senior management or its holding company, its subsidiaries and associates which may affect independence of the director...*"

Apart from the general statement above, there are certain specific factors that help determine the independence of directors.

However, Clause 49 does not outline the appointment procedure of independent directors, their qualifications, experience, their role/responsibility on the board, whom they represent (the company or the stakeholders) etc. The role and responsibility of the independent directors can be indirectly inferred from the role of the committees (such as remuneration committee, audit committee etc.) of which they are a part. This is a serious deficiency and hence results in ineffectiveness of independent directors on the board.

The Companies Act, 2013

The Companies Act, 2013 ('the new Act'), was notified on 30 August 2013 thereby replacing the Companies Act, 1956 (even though the Companies Act, 1956, has not been repealed by the new Act)

The erstwhile Companies Act, 1956, did not contain any provision with respect to independent directors. However, the new Act has identified the need for independent directors and therefore, incorporated detailed provisions with respect to definition of independent director, number of independent directors on the board, their term of office and remuneration. Further, the new Act also prescribes the manner of selection of independent directors through a data bank that is required to be maintained by anybody authorized by the Central Government and such databank would be displayed on the website of Ministry of Corporate Affairs. In addition, Schedule IV of the new Act provides 'Code for Independent Directors' which is mandatorily required to be followed by every company and the independent directors respectively. The said Schedule provides for guidelines of professional conduct, role, function and duties of the independent director, the process of appointment and evaluation mechanism of independent directors. It may also be noted that Draft Companies Rules 2013 (First Phase) issued by the Ministry of Corporate Affairs prescribes for qualification of independent directors being a person who possesses appropriate balance of skills, experience and knowledge in one or more fields of finance, law, management, sales, marketing, administration, research, corporate governance, technical operations or other disciplines related to the company's business.

Need for Independent Directors in PSEs and their Role

Having discussed in detail the evolution of independent directors and their legal status in India, it is most important to understand why do we need independent directors in CPSEs and why have we so spontaneously, yet gradually, risen to the belief that such directors are the key to 'good governance'.

CPSEs have a very complex and a heterogeneous board structure—functional directors on one hand, who are the 'domain knowledge carriers' and consider themselves supreme in the sphere of knowledge and information about the company as they believe they are the 'last and the best word' on the technical aspects of the company. However, they generally lack the interconnectedness between strategy and vision for efficient operation of the company. On the other hand, the board has the government nominee directors who are civil servants (generally from administrative ministry) possessing superb intellect and serving the socio-economic agenda of the government on the board. Therefore, their efforts are drawn towards aligning the board proceedings with the ownership policy. Absence of a clear ownership policy results in exerting and promoting undue influence on the board's decision leading to lack of 'connection' of the government nominee directors with the management and the board as a whole. Board generally gets tilted towards what the highest authority desires, i.e. the Government (through the government nominee directors) so as to fulfil their socio-economic agenda and any other agenda because of extraneous reasons.

In between the two are the independent directors who are experts in their own areas of work and supposed to bring an external and independent judgment on the board. They are neither wedded to the commercial orientation of the functional directors nor represent the political or social agenda of the government nominee directors. Therefore, it can be said that the role of independent directors is derived from the fundamental of 'impartiality' as their presence in the boardroom can ensure right balance between individual, economic and social interests of an organization. They contribute to the board by monitoring the company strategies and policies and challenging them constructively to serve the twin objective of safeguarding the interest of the Stakeholders and the Enterprise. Their role is to apply one's own judgment so as to ensure sufficiency of fairness, transparency and ethical way of consideration.

Challenges for Independent Directors

Despite improved legislations and regulations, the 'stand and status' of independent directors is questionable in the Indian corporate including CPSEs. This can be seen from the fact that in a survey conducted by FICCI and Grant Thornton in 2009 ('the survey'), 56% of the 500 (mid-market listed) responding companies did not have any committee/board in place for the purpose of appointment of independent directors on their board. A more worrying situation exists in the CPSEs where at present there are approximately 200 vacant positions for independent directors. Further, as of quarter ended September 2012, of 25 CPSEs that do not have the required number of independent directors, 7 belong to the oil and gas sector.

This is a very striking fact to be digested by the second most populated country in the world. This reflects that the process of appointing independent directors in CPSEs is not robust neither can be called impartial. The inefficiency on part of the respective ministries and Search Committee leads to a laggard situation for CPSEs wherein they are unable to take time-bound decision on account of absence of required number of independent directors. This can be seen from the fact that one of the biggest CPSE in India has not had a single independent director since August 2013 resulting in pendency of major decisions like purchase of expensive equipment, rising dues, appointment of suppliers in the company, etc. Also, it may be worth highlighting that as per a leading newspaper, for the quarter ended September 2012, 25 leading CPSEs did not have independent directors on their board due to non-initiation of proposals for appointment of such directors by their respective administrative ministry. Another critical challenge being faced by the independent directors is with respect to their role. Where the role of independent director should be that of 'oversight, insight and foresight', only 22% of the responding companies in the survey felt that the role played by the director in their company was substantial as against 59% of the respondent companies who felt that the involvement of independent directors in the annual planning and strategy development was moderate while in the case of 13% it was minimal. This is a deviation from the fact that 'monitoring' function has been the mainstay of evolution of independent Directors.

Thanks to the new Companies Bill (now Act), the duties and responsibility and accountability of Independent Directors have been defined.

With a dynamic environment it is imperative for the board of every company to be updated not only about the changing business environment but also of the possible solutions around them. This is only possible through regular training programs. However, a very disappointing fact came in light through India Corporate Governance Survey, 2006, wherein it was found that only 13% of the responding companies had some form of director training program in place. Another important factor contributing to board success is its performance evaluation. However, as per India Corporate Governance Survey 2006, only 25% of the responding companies had some form of evaluation process for non-executive directors. For CPSEs, the policies and procedures are framed by their administrative ministries and DPE. However, besides legal provisions in SEBI or Companies Act, there is neither a mandate by the Government for training of directors nor a formal code of conduct for performance evaluation of their directors (including independent directors). In addition, as discussed above the board of CPSEs constitutes of functional directors and government nominee directors making the size of the board generally large. On top of it the requirement of 50% independent directors on the Board further makes the functioning of the Boards unwieldy. Their agenda takes too long time to get through because the duration of the meetings is directly proportional to the number of Board members. In CPSEs the Parkinson's law that 'work multiplies accordingly to the number of persons deployed' holds true as it has been observed that at times objections/reservations are raised while passing Board agenda for various reasons, which often leads to unwarranted delay and may result in a casualty.

Way Forward

With the challenges and obstacles in their way, it would not be incorrect or unfair to say that independent directors can play an impactful role in the matrix of corporate governance only if both legal and corporate systems and practices enable such role. The legal systems, though important and vital for the role to be defined, are external to the PSEs environment, however, it is imperative that practices and systems which are more internal to the PSE world should be developed and directed towards providing effectiveness to independent directors.

Simplified Appointment Procedure

SEBI initiated action in 2007 against several government companies for non-compliance of Clause 49 on account of failure to appoint the requisite number of independent Directors. However, the actions were subsequently dropped by SEBI on the ground that, in the case of the government companies involved, the appointment of Directors is made by the President of India (as the controlling shareholder), acting through the relevant administrative ministry. SEBI found that despite continuous follow up by the respective companies, the appointments did not take effect due to the need to follow the requisite appointment process and hence the failure by those companies to comply with Clause 49 was not deliberate or intentional. This episode may have deleterious consequences on corporate governance reforms in India as compliance or otherwise of norms by government companies has an important signalling effect to the corporate at large.

At present, independent directors for a 'Ratna' CPSE (i.e. Maharatna, Navratna and Mini-Ratna) are recommended by the administrative ministry to the Public Enterprise Selection Board (PESB). The selection is then made by a 'Search Committee' which includes the Chairman of PESB,

Secretary, DPE, Secretary of the administrative ministry and four non-official members. The list of shortlisted candidates is then sent to the administrative ministry and finally to the Appointment Committee of Cabinet (ACC) through Minister in charge of the administrative Ministry for approval. It has been observed that Minister in charge has his/her own considerations.

The entire selection process as outlined above generally takes a long time in making the current practice very time consuming and not free from political interference. This jeopardizes the 'autonomous character' of independent directors resulting in loss of sanctity of the selection process. Consultation of administrative ministry, both at the time of proposing names of the plausible candidates and final approval results in appointment of 'dependable' independent Directors against the requirement of 'independent' Directors.

The responsibility assigned to an independent director is just like a 'double-barrelled gun' which can be used to both protect the excellence in governance and also destroy it. There is need for a simplified and transparent system of appointment of independent directors where no one is able to influence the autonomous character of such directors. There is a need to appoint independent directors through an independent body away from administrative ministry thereby minimizing any kind of political interference. This is in line with international practices being started in countries like China, Vietnam, Malaysia, etc., and developed countries where an independent body monitors every aspect of state-owned enterprise including selection of top management executives.

It is important and beneficial that all the board members are trained. It is specifically true for independent directors as they are the ones who need to provide an independent oversight and represent all stakeholders. Therefore, it is extremely important that independent directors are provided a platform where they are able to share and gather perspective and in turn generate a phenomenal thought process. The programs should be modus operandi for the resource persons and participants to explore and come with ideas that can be implemented while on the job. Training for independent directors should focus on effective leadership skills, corporate strategy and vision and most importantly how to voice their positions effectively in situations where other factors are proving to be more influential.

A beginning of the same has already been made where DPE's own Corporate Governance Guidelines call for board training. Further, Ratna companies have begun to offer director training in collaboration with SCOPE through programs like director's conclave for CMD and directors, CEO conference, director's certification program for new and potential directors. These programs are a good start and have helped raise awareness and capacity of directors to function effectively. However, more needs to be done.

Accountability Through Performance Evaluation

It has been reiterated that independent directors are cornerstones of corporate governance. However, since they are 'autonomous' and are not required to report to any particular authority on the board, it is imperative that they should be made accountable for their performance through a regular evaluation process by independent expert consultants of repute. This would also give them an incentive to carry out their roles more diligently. Incidentally there is no universal code of conduct to evaluate performance of independent directors. This suggests that independent directors are often brought on board ritualistically merely to comply with the legal requirement rather than with a view of obtaining any significant value addition. An attempt has been made in the Companies Act, 2013, wherein Schedule IV provides for performance evaluation of the independent directors by the entire board prior to renewal of term of office. However, a lot more needs to be done in terms of determining factors and matrix on the basis of which such directors would/should be evaluated. The parameters should be practical and consistent with the role and responsibility of the said directors and attempt to benchmark their position with respect to corporate behaviour. It is imperative that performance evaluation for the directors on the board should be benchmarked in respect of corporate behaviour with respect to ethical behaviour, integrity and fairness and strategy formulation, implementation and monitoring. Hence, there is a need to develop universal Code of Conduct for independent directors taking into consideration the experience in the past and also by sharing similar experience abroad. Some exercise has already been done in this respect by the DPE and PESB by taking view of the Government (being the major stakeholder) but it will not be complete unless the views/inputs are taken from other stakeholders like various departments, CEOs of CPSEs, academicians, researchers, etc. Yet another key obstacle to the proper functioning of independent directors relates to the availability of information from the board. Although the amount of information being shared with independent directors has been increasing over the years, there is still a need for drastic improvement both in terms of the timeliness and quality of information provided.

Also, it is essential that the role of independent directors should be crystallized and not subject to uncertainty. Though the new Companies Act, 2013, has brought about clarity on this aspect by enumerating the functions and duties of independent directors, however, the functioning should not just be limited to advising but extended to monitoring as well. The independent directors should, and need, to bring value on the board in terms of their ability to provide inputs on various aspects and also carry out a 'watch dog' function to protect interests of all stakeholders. Further, the size of the Board should be appropriate—i.e. neither too small nor too large thereby leading to timely and quick decisions, saving time and effort of the Board.

Independent Directors—Part of Effective Corporate Governance

Independence is in contaxt with law, ethics and integrity. While law does play an important role in creating the conditions for institutions like independent directors, the success of that institution depends largely on the individuals that occupy that position and systems that govern such individuals. An important role in this is played by the public sector as strict adherence to norms by PSEs may persuade others to follow as well. On the other hand, violation by PSEs (or by administrative ministries in operating the PSEs) is bound to trigger negative consequences in the corporate world at large thereby making implementation of corporate governance norms a more arduous task. Attention may be drawn that independent directors alone is not the answer to effective corporate governance. Epitomizing independent directors as the sole guardian of corporate governance creates a false sense of security amongst stakeholders. Therefore, it is necessary to understand that though this institution is not the only one but it is an important factor contributing to corporate governance. Where it is a concept providing connectivity to and alignment with corporate governance, it also needs to be combined with other attributes for a complete solution. Trend in international and experience thereof is a matter of further reform.

Independent External Monitors (IEMs)

Independent External Monitors (IEMs) are required to undertake an independent and an objective review of the obligations of both the parties Integrity Pact and the extent to which the same have been complied with by them.

Integrity Pact (IP)

Integrity Pact (IP) is understood as a vigilance tool through which the parties (buyer known as the 'Principal' and seller known as the 'Counterparty' or the 'Bidder') to the procurement contract enter into a separate agreement thereby committing each other not to exercise any corrupt influence on any aspect of the contract entered/proposed to be entered by them.

IP is voluntary but once adopted by any Principal, is binding for all its procurement contracts above a pre-determined threshold value of the said contract. Therefore, only those bidders, who have materialized IP with the Principal, would be considered as competent to participate in the bidding process.

Generally, IPs are entered between any public authority (being the 'Principal') and the counterparty being vendors/ bidders.

Vide Circular dated 18 May 2009, the Central Vigilance Commission (CVC) has laid down 'Standard Operating Procedures' (SOP) for adoption of IP in major Government Departments/organizations for their procurement contracts (i.e. the Government Department/organization is the Principal).

Further, the Department of Public Enterprises (DPE) has issued an Office Memorandum on 9 September 2011 wherein directions have been given to all CPSEs to enter into IP for all their procurement transactions/contracts (above a prescribed threshold limit) identified by the said CPSEs in consultation with financial advisors of their respective administrative ministries. This implies the CPSEs would be the Principal for all their procurement contracts where IP is to be entered into with the bidder.

Qualities of IEMs

The IEM should be independent and committed wherein he should be able to objectively monitor with 'intentions for public good'.

The IEM should possess strength of character and impeccable behaviour.

He should be able to add value to the project and should be better equipped to uncover/identify malpractices and corruption thereby increasing his accountability to all parties to the contract.

Appointment of IEMs

The names for panel of IEMs for procurement contracts would be recommended by the organization (in consultation with CVO) and approved by the CVC.

An individual can hold position of IEM in maximum two organizations.

Initial tenure of appointment is 3 years, extendable by 2 years on receipt of request by the CVC from the organization appointing the IEM. However, total term of IEM cannot exceed a period of 5 years in an organization.

Number of IEMs: Navratna PSE - 3, whereas in Other PSEs - 2.

Organizations generally propose a panel of more than 3 names to the CVC for consideration. For PSEs having a large territorial spread or those having multiple subsidiaries, more IEMs could be appointed but at no point in time there should be more than 2 IEMs for a single subsidiary. At the time of appointment as IEM, the person should be less than 70 years of age. Further, if on completion of initial tenure of 3 years, the age has crossed 70 years, extension of 2 years shall not be admissible. Remuneration payable to IEMs shall be equivalent to that payable to an independent director in the said organization. Terms and conditions for appointment (including remuneration payable) should be communicated separately to the IEM and not provided for in the IP or the notice inviting tenders.

Qualification of IEMs

The proposed names should be persons of high integrity and experience.

While recommending the names of the IEMs, detailed bio-data of the candidates is also provided to the CVC. Such bio data should outline the details of postings before superannuation (if the proposed IEM has worked in the government sector, then details with respect to postings during last 10 years prior to superannuation should also be included), special achievements, experience, etc. It would be desirable that the candidates should possess domain experience of the organizations' activities and other relevant fields. CVC considers names for appointment as IEM of only those individuals who have retired from top management positions in Government of India Departments or PSEs. Any individual who is either serving or retired from an organization would not be considered for appointment as IEM in the same organization. Eminent persons and executives of private sector may also be considered for appointment as IEM by CVC.

Role of IEMs

IEMs are primarily responsible to oversee the implementation of IPs in order to prevent corruption, bribes and other unethical practices that may create any kind of undue influence on the Principal thereby affecting the procurement contract. They review and provide expert feedback on all documents and steps of the procurement process (beginning from notice inviting tender till the final execution of the contract). The IEMs are responsible for monitoring access to information pertaining to the contract and hence, would have access to all contract documents whenever required. The IEMs are required to meet the Chief Executive of the organization on a regular basis in order to discuss and review the information on tenders awarded in the previous period/month and the progress on the same. They ensure examination of complaints (pertaining to the contract) received by them from the bidders and would be responsible for communicating their views/recommendations to the CEO of the organization (being the Principal) in a time-bound manner. In case, the complaint/suspicion is that of a serious irregularity requiring legal/administrative action, the IEM may also send his report directly to the CVO and the CVC. They would also be required to coordinate with other anti-corruption agencies such as CVC and if required engage services of outside agencies (like accounting firms, law firms, etc.) in order to discharge his responsibilities. The IEM's prime responsibility is to keep the public and authorities informed and thereby contribute to raise overall confidence in the organization. This can be achieved by making the reports of the IEMs public.

Salient Features

IEMs would have the right to attend any meeting between the Principal and the Counterparties. They also have the right to attend internal meetings of the Principal which may pertain to the contract for which they have been appointed. Ideally, the panel of IEMs should meet at least once in two months in order to take stock of the ongoing tendering process. The recommendations of the IEMs would be advisory in nature without any legal binding. However, they should not be understood as consultants to the Management and hence, advice once tendered would not be subject to review. The Notice Inviting Tenders should name at least one IEM but any complaint/matter of concern should be examined by the entire *panel of IEMs*. The role of the CVO would not be affected by that of the IEM. A matter that is being examined by the IEM may also be examined by the CVO if received by him or directed to him by the CVC. The CVO shall examine the complaint in terms of the provisions of the CVC Act or Vigilance Manual.

Challenges (as outlined by TII)

There appears to be lack of clarity of the role of IEM vis-à-vis CVO and there is lack of clarity whether IEM should be proactive and act as advisors and crisis managers for the business or they should respond only on receipt of complaints. Sometimes, it has been observed that non availability of logistics support from the management hinders functioning of IEMs. Sometimes it is also felt that vendors are hesitant to complain to IEMs on account of fear of reprisal resulting in communication gap between the IEM and the vendors. Many private companies are hesitant to sign IPs especially on account of wariness with the role of IEMs as they would prefer IEMs to be persons from within their organizations.

Recommendations (as outlined by TII)

There should be Uniform orientation training programs for IEMs, and CVC must define and clarify the role and responsibility of IEMs taking into consideration the past experiences of working of IP. Also, FAQ on roles and responsibilities of IEMs may also be developed. CVC must be requested to make placing of IEMs report in board meetings mandatory. IEMs should hold quarterly review meetings in order to leverage their functioning.

A list of references and various circulars on IEM is in **Appendix – II.**

BEST LEADERS – WORST LEADERSHIP

There is marked difference between leader and leadership. Leader refers to a person who occupies the position of CEO in PSEs. Therefore, leader is centred towards role in a person. Quality of leader is centred towards his individual skill including his behavioural attitude, aptitude, socializing and network whereas leadership is a system-driven process and it does not depend on an individual characteristic in entirety. It is a complex communication involving leaders and followers and depends upon interpersonal skill and team building. It is essentially to develop collective leadership for better organization and bringing excellence in them. Therefore, leadership refers to organizational competence which requires proper interaction within a team across various layers (both inter and intra) in an organization. Leadership also requires horizontal as well as vertical communication between different layers. It is centred for building a sustainable system in the organization through collaborative innovation. It is also not true that leadership can be superimposed to all countries because it is rather contextual, cultural and interpersonal and these differ from country to country. In India interpersonal and hierarchical needs are greater than Western countries. Leaders in PSEs are more "conformance" oriented as compared to "performance" and, therefore, they work on the philosophy of direction from the owner or regulatory bodies compared to decisiveness on their own. Whereas, the leader seeks his best on his style and behavioural competence and not from their skill, experience or marked knowledge alone, this approach is not found in Western leaders as they are used to system-oriented process. Therefore, leaders must develop capacity and ability to adapt to the fast changing environment, innovate and excel by adopting a system-oriented process and not superimpose their personal attributes on his subordinates. A comparison of leader vs. leadership is given in the table below:

Attributes	Leadership	Leader's Attributes
Have	Followers	Subordinates
Horizon	Long-term	Short-term
Seeks	Vision	Objectives
Decision	Facilitates	Makes
Appeal to	Heart	Head
Power	Personal Charisma	Formal authority
Culture	Shapes	Enacts
Style	Transformational	Transaction
Likes	Striving	Action
Exchange	Excitement for work	Money for work
Wants	Achievement	Results
Rules	Breaks	Makes
Conflict	Uses	Avoids
Truth	Seeks	Establishes
Concern	What is right	Being right
Blame	Takes	Blames
Credit	Gives	Takes
Persuasion	Sell	Tell
Essence	Change	Stability
Focus	Leading people	Managing work
Approach	Sets direction	Plans detail
Energy	Passion	Control
Dynamic	Proactive	Reactive
Risk	Takes	Minimizes
Direction	New roads	Existing roads

Based on the above, we find that Indian corporate CEOs in public sector are best leaders but possess poor leadership quality. They have to change their style to bring professional leadership.

Leadership would require clarity with regard to owner's policy and Board's responsibility, their performance evaluation against benchmarked positions and power structure.

Leadership Trends and Challenges

Leadership is a quality, an essential ingredient that shapes the present as well as the future and is never out of fashion or demand. Rather, the constant demand for it over ages reflects a basic human and societal need to have a strong set of norms and values to function effectively in a civilized manner. Historically, we have had many exemplary leaders to learn from. Be it in the political, socio-economic, academic or religious/spiritual arenas, these leaders have shaped the world. However, the concept of leadership, his ability to be a leader or lead is an abstract from which we need to understand. The natural aptitude and his competency can be acquired and polished over the course of time through appropriate education and training.

In as much as it is something that can be imbibed from proper training, or appropriate specialized programmes, courses or methods, we have a huge responsibility of investing in leaders of today and tomorrow. And we do have increased interest generated in this area. But the trends in leadership are changing. The global economic recession of 2007 set in motion a domino effect which led to a disruption of the fundamentals of economies across the globe. The environment has become more complex and challenging. The ground rules have gone for an overhaul and the time lag before any path becomes clear has made leaders and the leadership an intimidating choice.

Changes in Environment

The environment has become increasingly dynamic, dealing with changes which are in constant turbulence. Uncertainty, volatility, ambiguity are all adding to the complexity. A large number of interacting elements are continuously emerging and the number of variables in each equation has increased. Interactions among these different variables had become non-linear and tightly coupled so that small changes lead to disproportionately large effects. Moreover, even though the technology has advanced, the information system has become taut resulting in 'information overload'. This makes the information set available at any point of time incomplete and sometimes indecipherable. New technologies also disrupt old work practices.

Leadership quality in leaders would require:

- ✓ Adaptability
- ✓ Self-Awareness
- ✓ Boundary spanning
- ✓ Collaboration
- ✓ Network thinking
- ✓ Creativity
- ✓ Comfortable with ambiguity
- ✓ Complex "thinking" abilities
- ✓ Learning agility
- ✓ Strategic thinking.

The Decline of the Heroic Leader – the Rise of Collective Leadership

Often, a repeated argument/point about growing complexity in our environment makes it quite clear that no one person can know the solutions to all problems or even identify the problem itself. It is humanly impossible. Collaboration between all stakeholders is essential, each of whom hold a different aspect of reality. We must acknowledge this shift in leadership incumbencies from individual to groups. New era of leadership and the trend deal with managing complexities in our environment which is a major challenge. However, we also should be open to look and experiment with new processes in leadership development.

Leaders play a major role in the matrix of corporate governance. Confluence of corporate leadership with corporate governance codes and norms is essential in leading the enterprises and business houses towards strengthening national and global capital markets, protecting investors and enhancing competitiveness. Investors over the world, pay a large premium for companies with good leadership as these have positive impact on their image. The essence of the corporate governance is leadership development. It has been increasingly realized that effective leadership developed through a system-oriented process would raise the bar on governance standard of the corporate world.

Developing a Leadership Pipeline

Indian corporates are continuously expanding their reach nationally and internationally. Rapid expansion and exponential growth have left the companies in a deep need of capacity building and talent pool. The growth of talent pool has not kept pace with the requirement as they are experiencing a significant leadership shortfall to fill their senior level. A recent survey reports that supply is limited because many individuals are lacking critical skills resulting in talent scarcity across important sectors. Spotting potential leaders, from entry level in their careers and nurturing them has become increasingly essential. A robust and sustainable leadership needs to be developed to ensure that they have required skills and knowledge to deliver economic value.

Leadership is about engaging and developing the talented people on a systematic basis and not just when a position becomes vacant or is created. Continuous engagement would help in maintaining a pool of potential candidates who would be able to step into senior leadership roles, even at the Middle or Senior management levels successfully. It is necessary, therefore, to have a strategy in place to identify the potential executives and focus on preparing them for larger leadership roles. It is equally important for leader to make sure that the "right people are in the right roles" in tune with the concept of the "Role-Person Match". While an organization's Head or Top Leader is ultimately responsible for steering its Business and Strategy, successful leadership quality would require capacity building of their Manager at every level to keep a constant eye on Potential Talent. Leadership can also be developed by strengthening the connection between and alignment of the efforts of individual leaders and the systems through which they influence organizational operations. This indicates differentiation between leader development and leadership development. Leader development focuses on the development of the leader such as his/her personal attributes viz. honesty, humility, trustworthiness, competent and compassionate.

Ethical Leadership and Values

Ethics is the sine qua non for best practices in corporate governance. Increasingly, leaders of business are now waking up to the reality of Organizational Ethics and Social Responsibility. Ethical behaviour is integral to the existence of any company and it strengthens the investor's confidence by ensuring the company's commitment to higher growth and profits on a sustained basis. On the other hand, Unethical behaviour affects individuals, work teams and organizational productivity and performance as well as the brand image of the company.

Public Sector Enterprises and Leadership Development

Excellence in leadership has always been the fundamental prerequisite for PSEs. They have produced many of the best leaders for the country in line with the Government Policy of "Economic Growth with Social Justice". Sustained good performance of PSEs over the years demonstrates the strength and competitiveness of leadership in these companies. Their inclination to leadership excellence will help them in successfully encountering challenges posed by increased competition from domestic private corporates, multinational Companies (MNCs) coming to India as well as exploring new markets abroad. Today, PSEs stand for creating value and examples but there should be a perfect integration of ethical leadership and corporate governance reflecting upon organizational performance.

Top management personnel, chairman-cum-managing-director and directors compose the top-rung leadership in PSEs. Public Enterprises Selection Board (PESB) set up with the objective of evolving a sound managerial policy for CPSEs, advises Government on appointments of their top management posts. The policy is to appoint outstanding professional managers through a fair and objective selection procedure. Government has also recognized the need to develop a cadre of professional managers within Public Sector. Hence unless markedly better candidates are available from outside, internal candidates employed in these PSEs are preferred. PSEs have also made extensive efforts to enrich their human capital through skill development, attitudinal change and team building. They have groomed technical and managerial talent in various core and vital industries of the country. This in turn generated a critical mass of talent which acted as a base for the industry at large.

PSEs recruit talented young people generally through open competition. As a result of Human Resource policies, the Indian PSEs are in the vanguard of productivity enhancement. With less manpower, their value additions, turnover, profits, etc., are increasing. PSEs' goal-oriented HRM strategies are evident in most leading CPSEs—SAIL, CIL, ONGC, BHEL, IOC, NTPC, GAIL, Power Grid, HPCL, EIL, RITES, NHPC among several others. Thus the human resources churned by PSEs have provided a direct and indirect boost for economic growth.

Here it is pertinent to refer to a study of Ernst and Young on "Government as Best in Class Shareholders", according to which a majority of Indian and Saudi Arabian citizens consider managers in State Owned Enterprises (SOEs) better than their counterparts in private enterprises. The study says, "It seems that SOEs Managers inefficiency is a pervasive belief, both at global level and individual level. Interestingly, however, for the two countries where the perception of service quality of SOEs is unusually positive (India and Saudi Arabia), a majority believes that managers in SOEs are better than in private firms". In particular, the Indian "Navratnas" and their professional and autonomous management have registered positive recognition by citizens, according to the study. The need of the hour is to develop best leadership and not only leaders as we have best leaders but worst leadership.

CORPORATE SOCIAL RESPONSIBILITY – PSEs PERSPECTIVE

Corporate Social Responsibility (CSR), voluntary or legal compliance of social and ecological responsibility has become an increasingly important activity in the corporate sector world over. The concept of 'CSR' gained worldwide popularity courtesy growing media and political coverage of the long term impact of such a policy on the theory of sustainable development. The IT revolution expedited access to information and consumers educated themselves under bloggers' watchful eyes. Customers, sociologists, economists, environmentalists, all became interested in and theorized about a corporation's impact on society and environment. Quite interestingly, even the corporate world sat up and took notice of how potent a tool CSR could be in terms of image building. They acknowledged the expenses made thus on CSR as investments and had ample opportunity to test the validity of such investments in recessionary periods. A lot many firms had their sailing comparatively easy in recession given the trust and goodwill earned on account of their CSR initiatives. Besides, with the accelerated pace of globalization and emerging ecological issues, many organizations progressively realized their broader responsibility towards society and environment and the benefits of providing CSR programmes in and around their locations. They have realized that a strong CSR programme is an essential element in nurturing good business practices and balanced growth of society. It also adds to their image which ultimately gets converted to a better bottom-line. Here it is pertinent to mention that CSR has been a forte of the public sector.

The roots of the concept of CSR can be traced to many religious scriptures that encourage people to share their fortunes with the under-privileged. In India also the concept of CSR is not new as charity and service have been a hallmark of Indian culture while business involvement in social welfare and development has been the tradition. Big business families all along have been donating generously for social causes by setting up charitable foundations, educational and healthcare institutions and trusts for community development. The underlying idea behind 'trusteeship in business' propounded by the Father of Nation Mahatma Gandhi centred primarily around the thinking that different leaders of business are the custodians of wealth of society and it is their responsibility to put it to best use of the society.

Over the years, the face of charity or philanthropy has changed and evolved as Corporate Social Responsibility. It has now become a fundamental business practice and has gained much attention from Chief Executives, Board of Directors and Management Teams of large companies. Societal expectations have prompted them to redefine their role and responsibility with respect to corporate performance measured in terms of economic impact, social impact and environmental impact, commonly called 'Triple Bottom-line'.

Since inception, PSEs have played a leading role in fulfilling social obligations. Set up with the twin objectives of economic development with social justice, these enterprises have assigned a high priority to the ideals of CSR. They have made massive investments in industrial and social infrastructure of the country. PSEs have rendered yeoman service in areas of their operations. In fact, it is a matter of pride that their CSR strategies are aligned to national priorities to meet the basic needs of citizens like literacy enhancement, educational aids, providing drinking water, community development and infrastructure, environment protection, health care and family welfare. To bring parity in the society, PSEs are earmarking a part of their CSR budget for the weaker section with special focus on the SC/ST and backward communities. Scholarship schemes are there to promote education in the localities. In addition to that, government owned companies have also instituted meritorious scholarships to enhance the emphasis on promoting education for the girl child. The aim and objective of CSR for various CPSEs are initiation of developmental activities in the neglected areas, supporting ecology, environment conservation and disaster relief. PSEs have also responded magnificently and generously at the time of need. As and when natural calamities like earthquake, cyclonic storm, flood, drought, etc., have struck, causing huge loss of life, property and hardship to the survivors, public enterprises have always helped in alleviating the sufferings of the affected people.

For example, a cloudburst occurring in Leh caused tragic loss of life and unprecedented devastation. Many PSEs once again came forward and extended all possible help to overcome the miseries of the affected people. Hindustan Prefab Ltd did an incredible work in this regard. It constructed 170 one-room prefab houses in a record time of 41 days and further 280 prefab houses were constructed in different locations. There are numerous examples where PSEs have made a significant difference in the society and improved the overall quality of life of people.

Guidelines on Corporate Social Responsibility

The activities under CSR are selected in such a manner that the benefits reach the smallest unit, i.e. village panchayat, block or district depending upon the operations and resource capability of the enterprises. Under these guidelines the CPSEs are required to move from an ad-hoc approach to the project mode with specified time frames and periodic milestones. The activities undertaken under CSR should also be in consonance and consultation with State Governments, District Administrations, Local Administrations as well as Central Government Departments/Agencies, Self-Help Groups, etc., to avoid duplication.

Social Audit of CSR Activities

In recent times, a social impact evaluation has assumed major significance. Through social audit, a balance can be achieved between the need of community and CSR contribution of corporates to fulfil those needs. SCOPE has been emphasizing the need for social audit of the expenses incurred on CSR activities to introduce check and balance and to confirm that CSR expenses do not become a subject of criticism of PSEs as well as private corporates. Social audit will also ensure that the CSR funds are not diverted to those who do not have credential/credibility up to the mark. As there has been mushroom growth of NGOs in the country, organization should be very careful while selecting them for implementation of their CSR Projects. There is also need to assess as to whether the CSR allocation is reaching the end-users or not.

Extend Mandatory CSR Component to all Corporates

In public enterprises, there is Board approved Policy for CSR and proposals for allocation of funds is generally within the approved policy which are also subjected to number of checks and balances.

SCOPE has strongly advocated that industry fraternity should contribute towards corporate social responsibility as a corporate citizen and has urged that the mandatory provision for CSR be extended to private corporates also. Given the socio-economic condition of our country, where more than 70% of people still live in villages and are confronted with abject poverty, it should be the prime concern for all the corporates, whether public or private to discharge their CSR as a part of nation building. If the benefits of rising economic development do not reach the society, it will be difficult to sustain their brand and corporates will find it difficult to survive.

PSEs have been harping on mandatory 2% contribution by all corporates. This is required because private enterprises are also implemented based on investment which is tax-payers' money only. Financial institutions and banks also provide the resource based on tax-payers money. Frankly speaking, all money is public money unless it is black money. Therefore, there is need for level playing for both Public and Private Sector.

ONE CODE FOR SUSTAINABLE DEVELOPMENT

Social responsibility is coded into the DNA of PSEs. However, more often than not, the social objectives become a constraint on PSEs, putting them at a disadvantage vis-à-vis private players. The point is that should the responsibility of sustainable development be shouldered solely by the PSEs?

Corporate Social Responsibility (CSR) is a vital component of Sustainable development (SD). The two have become integral to business. Rights and responsibilities go hand in hand for all businesses, and are ownership-neutral. The challenge in the Indian context lies in furthering CSR as a major tool, stripping it of its vagueness and establishing its strong network with sustainable development. Once clarity is achieved, it should be encased in legality to be enforceable, so that the entire corporate body follows a single code of conduct to move in the same direction.

The Hurdles

What exactly are the hindrances? For starters, the association of competitive advantage with sustainability needs to be exhaustively researched, debated and advertised/ popularized as an infallible business method. Secondly, it should be acknowledged, through studies, that the voluntary aspects of SD are inadequate to address the global contingencies since they lack proper structure.

Many reform-oriented, resilient, adaptable and sturdy public enterprises are based on the sustainable development theme. The Department of Public Enterprises gives 'sustainable development' a weightage of 5% in its annual assessment of CPSEs. The annual evaluation reveals that the CPSEs are improving their score on meeting annual targets. Also remarkable is the symmetry PSEs have attained between people, planet and profits, as there is a rise in the number of PSEs that have continuously posted profits while pursuing the triple bottom-line approach.

Examples abound of PSEs that have meshed sustainability into their core business. Bharat Petroleum has been involved in various health, education and environment conservation related activities. A community development programme of BPCL in village Ramthenga of Orissa, has made explicit the company's social commitments. Its focus has been on education, health with respect to hazards, sanitation and safeguards of working in mines.

Strong integration between all groups is central to the theme of sustainable development. Rural India deserves special attention here since India lives in its villages. Some 62 crore rural people, especially women, are waiting for Corporate India to come and do their bit in key areas like health, education, sanitation, drinking water and overall living standard. If given proper attention, rural India can become the biggest catch for sustainable development. PSEs have to once again play the role model here.

RTI: TIME TO WIDEN ITS AMBIT

The Right to Information (RTI) Act 2005 has brought about perceptible change in terms of greater transparency, accountability and wider participation of various stakeholders in decision-making – an ultimate tenet of a democratic development process. The Act serves as an instrument of effective governance and inclusive growth by increasing people's participation, improving delivery mechanisms and reaching benefits to the targeted beneficiaries more effectively. Under the RTI any citizen can request information from a "public authority", which is bound to furnish the same. The Act has brought greater accountability and transparency in the government sector. Time has come to explore whether the scope and area of the RTI action need to be widened.

As many as 18 countries have already brought the private sectors under some version of the RTI Act. Though the legislative ambit varies from country to country, generally all those who do public services, including social services, have been brought under the Act. These countries are South

Africa, Angola. Armenia, Colombia, the Czech Republic, the Dominican Republic, Estonia, Finland, France, Iceland, Liechtenstein, Panama, Poland, Peru, Turkey, Trinidad and Tobago, Slovakia and the UK. The public information Act of Estonia, for example, covers state and local agencies and private entity conducting public duties, including education, healthcare, social and public service.

In India, the social sector, which has seen a mushrooming growth of non-governmental organizations (NGO), must also be brought under the RTI Act, as the operations and funding of many of them are not transparent and out of public domain. A social audit of NGOs may reveal the true story in the social sector. Similarly, the non-government R&D sector has always been a subject of concern because of the tax-evasion in the name of R&D incentives. It would not be a bad idea to bring all the R&D expenditures, whether private or public, under the RTI Act. The concept 'Freedom of Information' found embodiment in India in the form of Right to Information Act. The Act applies to all states and Union Territories (except J&K which is covered under a state-level law).

Today economic world has become far more complex with the distinction between private and public sector getting blurred. There is a range of investment from public institutions to some foreign wealth funds, in a large private sector company. Then there is also growing need for public-private partnerships (PPPs) in infrastructure and socially relevant sectors. This transformation, as well as growing incidence of corruption and misuse of public money, calls for introducing relevant changes in the laws and regulations governing the industrial sector. Since the public sector is already subject to public accountability and scrutiny, the same needs to be extended to the private sector. Besides promoting good governance ethics, public accountability would also ensure judicious use of public funds, thus ushering in efficiency and higher growth.

PSEs have always followed high standards of transparency and public accountability in their working in true spirit. The RTI Act and the institution of Central Information Commission have further strengthened the transparency and accountability and enhanced the good image of the PSEs. It has also helped in strengthening customer-orientation in products and designs and thus leading to judicious use of resources along with environment protection. In other words, by increasing efficiency and improving performance, RTI is helping the PSEs in optimizing economic returns on public investment. This perhaps calls for extending its ambit to include private sector and non-government organizations (NGOs) where large public funds are involved, for instance, public–private partnership projects. Time has also come to amend the Act itself based on the experience of implementing authorities, since its inception in 2005 to remove small deterrents and to improve its efficacy.

It should be noted that transparency, higher credibility and due diligence have now gained more importance than ever in the last few years. It is rather unfortunate that a number of monetary scandals have come to light in recent times involving huge public money. There has been lack of proper and timely scrutiny. Considering that India is a developing country that needs large amount of investible resources and faster economic development, such corruption incidences point to insurmountable economic loss.

In view of the benefits of RTI and the reasons for which it was introduced, mainly to remove secrecy from public decision-making and thus reduce incidence of undue benefit mongering and rampant corruption in public sphere, are equally valid for the private sector entities also. It is common knowledge that corruption is common to both public as well as private sector. In recent years, distinction between public and private sector has become more blurred with growing number of infrastructure projects being planned through Public-Private Partnership (PPP) mode. Since infrastructure projects require huge funds and have long gestation, involving both, the public and private sectors can make them more feasible as well as lead to faster progress.

Under such a scenario, it presents a very strong case to bring deterrents, checks and balances in private corporate sector as well, not only as a level playing between the two entities but also to clean the system of procurement and overall governance. Normally, the governments across the world tend to transfer public money and critical functions in private hands for PPP projects and even when privatization of public enterprises is taken up. Under such circumstances, where public money has changed hands from public to private, there must be adequate checks and balances to judge the fairness and ethical aspects between the public and private partners. There is also a need to sustain PPPs with the help of proper checks and balances through regulatory and policy mechanisms. As such, not only RTI but also proper audit including those from CAG may bring more transparency and accountability in the corporate sector in case of PPP as well as private model and thus help in curbing corruption.

The RTI Act today covers only the Government sector, including PSEs, broadly based on the premise that the sector uses 'public money'. RTI which was earlier considered as necessary evil has been gradually accepted, adopted and also appreciated by PSE as it has created a positive brand image of PSEs and has also improved the working behaviour of PSE employees. Hence for long-term sustainability of any project or service, it is very important that good corporate governance practices are followed. The increasing number of PPP projects and the rising public participation in equity issues on one hand and better outcome of such checks and balances make a strong case for extending the ambit of the RTI Act and also some of the other regulations like CAG to the non-government corporate sector. Extension of the RTI Act would not only further the objective of RTI to bring greater transparency and accountability to our economic/ commercial public-private life, but would also foster a system of increased responsibility towards citizen's overall welfare from all sectors. Similarly, all the non-government organizations (NGOs) need to be covered under the RTI Act. As NGOs which handle large public money are not covered under RTI, neither they are controlled through statutory/ regulatory norms as in case of Government organizations including PSEs. This lacuna many times results in corruption and wastage of funds.

India is a vast country that requires substantial investments in social sectors like health, education, basic amenities, etc. As most of these areas are still not covered under any statutory or regulatory framework, chances of malpractices leading to usurping of public funds are very high. The idea of extending public accountability to the private and social service sector is to encourage judicious use of resources and enhancing efficiencies in the system, thereby promoting faster, sustainable and balanced economic growth.

Besides expanding its reach, it is also important to introduce some amendments to the Act itself. Several years have passed, since the RTI Act was introduced and many aberrations now necessitate revisit of the Act to bring suitable changes. For instance, the Act in its present form allows a time frame of 30 days for responding to a query posed. In case of PSEs, some of which have operations in remote areas across the country, it has been found that collating all the information sometimes requires more than the stipulated period. Hence, it is suggested that this time frame should be extended to at least 45 days to make it more convenient and practical. Similarly, there is no clarity on number of questions covered under a single query, which many times put unnecessary pressure on the organization. It also leads to duplication of effort. It has been noticed that at times variety of questions are asked to harass the administration. Further a lot of undue benefits are derived by disgruntled elements to become bottleneck which are coming in the way of optimal performance. A lot of wastage of time in attending to larger number of enquiries/clarifications sought from vested interest has become a common feature. There is an element of cost in terms of time and efforts spent in addressing a RTI query. Almost 40000 queries before small CIC manpower also pose big problem to process such large queries. Efforts should be made to avoid or discourage use of RTI for wilful vendetta against a company or a person. There is also an issue of ascertaining or verifying credibility of a person who is seeking information using RTI. Some form of identity verification of a person like Adhaar ID or Pan Card Numbers should be made mandatory so that only genuine citizens of the country can access this Act. Therefore, the Institution of CIC needs to be strengthened as the manpower is insufficient to and not commensurate with number of inquiries received in CIC.

The public sector has gained tremendously by the implementation of RTI Act as its efficiency, performance and image have improved considerably. We would like this Act to be expanded further and made more industry-friendly.

PSEs GAINING COMPETITIVE EDGE THROUGH TECHNOLOGY UPGRADATION

Technology, R&D and Innovation are very important components of growth and performance in today's world of intense global competition. These should form part of activities of any competitive and progressive enterprise. India's expenditure on R&D is about 0.8% of GDP and Government envisages increasing it to 2% of GDP by the end of 12th Five Year Plan.

Public Sector Enterprises have served as nurseries of technology. They have nurtured a pool of management and technology talent which is now available in other sectors of national economy also. PSEs further need to accelerate in the areas of R&D and technology efficiency and help each other to achieve world class manufacturing facilities in the country. Unfortunately, in R&D & Technology

Development area India is placed much below the ladder whereas small countries have developed good technology and export to various countries including India.

Science and technology is the bedrock on which modern economic and vibrant enterprises have been built. To stay competitive in the face of globalised paradigm, the level of scientific and technological competence is an imperative.

Research and Development (R&D) enables assimilation of acquired technology and fuels upgradation and to impart innovativeness in the productive efforts of enterprises. Research is essentially basic or applied. While basic research creates new knowledge and critical breakthroughs, applied research essentially helps development of new uses of the acquired knowledge in enhancing productivity. Science and technology, leads to new innovation and product diversification and incremental values.

India over the years has attempted to attain impressive scientific and technological capabilities backed by R&D facilities. This is in particular true of India's central PSEs. India's first Prime Minister Jawaharlal Nehru had seen India emerging as an economic power on the back of science and technology. His implicit faith in service was reflected in *"Even more than present, the future belongs to science and to those who make friends with science and seek its help for advancement of humanity"*.

The first Industrial Policy Statement was issued in 1948 which envisaged adoption of new technological capability through acquisition, assimilation adoption and development. In 1983, the government issued the Technology Policy Statement, which provided specifically for in-house R&D units in industrial enterprises to interface with the national laboratories and educational institutions. Following the latter, the in-house units came under the purview of the Department of Scientific and Industrial Research (DSIR), under the Ministry of Science and Technology. As a result of the incentives and the liberalized environment, several industrial units, private and public—more public—established own in-house R&D units.

There are presently 1,313 recognized R&D units incurring expenditure of Rs 7600 crore a year. Of these, 20% belong to public and the joint sector, although the total number of the public enterprises is only a fraction of private enterprises.

Industry-wise Distribution of R&D Units

Industry	**R&D Units No.**
Chemicals & allied[a] industries	567
Electricals & electronics	272
Mechanical engineering	185
Processing industries[b]	155
Agro industries[c]	134
Total	**1313**

[a] includes drugs & pharmaceuticals and biotechnology
[b] includes metallurgical, refractory, paper, cement, ceramics, leather and others
[c] includes biotechnology and food processing

Out of the 1313 units, the in-house R&D units spending over Rs 5 crore a year number 151, while those spending between Rs 1 and 5 crore a year add up to 296. These 447 units spend a total of Rs 5782 crore, of which 34 units, less than 10%, from the public sector spend nearly Rs 1020 crore or over 17.6% of the total expenditure. It clearly is indicative of the greater concern of CPSEs for R&D activities.

Besides the in-house R&D units at thc industry level, the large network of R&D institutions in the private sector and ones sponsored by the ministries are engaged in extensive research for innovation and for upgradation and development of technologies. The government earmarked an estimated Rs 22,000 crore for various technology projects under government domain in 2009-10. An estimated 68,000 personnel are dedicated to these R&D units, with 3,500 holding doctoral degrees and 22,000 are either post-graduates or graduates.

While the public sector is playing a pivotal role in augmenting the technology in Indian industry through R&D effort, some selected private sector companies, such as Tata Motors, are also contributing handsomely to entrepreneurial effort in R&D. Tata Nano, wholly developed on the back of its R&D effort, has gained worldwide attention and accolades.

Overall Indian expenditure on R&D is estimated at less than a percent (0.8%) of the GDP. The R&D expenditure of most countries hovers around 1% of their GDP, including some among highly developed countries. The high spenders on R&D include Sweden (3.7%), Korea (3.5%), United States (2.7%) to name only a few. China's R&D expenditure averages 1.5% of its GDP. Government envisages increase in R&D investment to 2% of GDP by the public as well as the private sector corporates and institutions by the end of 12th Five Year Plan. To realize this, a package of measures is being put in place that covers:

- higher allocation to scientific research;
- setting up of new institutions for science, education and research;
- creation of centres of excellence and facilities in emerging and frontline areas in academic and national institutes;
- strengthening infrastructure for R&D in universities;
- encouraging public-private R&D partnerships; and
- giving grants for industrial R&D projects.

While the Government envisages increasing the R&D spending to 2% of the GDP, fresh incentives to encourage R&D in the economy have been announced. These include: enhancement of weighted deduction from income tax on expenditure incurred by in-house R&D units from 150% to 200%; enhancement from 125% to 175% of weighted deduction from income tax on payments made to National Laboratories, Universities or IITs or specified scientific individuals provided the said sum used for scientific research is under an approved programme; and, payments made to associations engaged in research approved under Income Tax

Act to be allowed as weighted deduction of 175%. The income of such approved research associations shall be exempt from tax.

The Public Sector in the Forefront of Technology Adoption

Under the theme, a vision for the new millennium, *India 2020* by Dr. APJ Abdul Kalam set out a new agenda for the public sector. While recognizing that "PSUs are technologically and managerially strong", it recognizes that "*the PSUs have done this country proud on a number of occasions*". It explains:

"We should remember that our country was not manufacturing even simple pins prior to independence. Thus today major industries to manufacture sophisticated equipment, machine tools, electronic products and defence machinery which was a dream some years back. Central PSUs have purchased technologies from abroad to put India firmly on the industrial map".

And India 2002 reminds us that

"The management of the PSUs are making an important contribution and are partnering PSE of another industry, or an industry in the small-scale or an R&D lab or MNC".

"Today, PSEs contribute in developing the technological core strengths of India. They work to transform the core strengths of the enterprise into wealth, which indirectly flows to the people. Such a targeted approach is pursued by each of the PSUs"

Exposed to the exigencies of globalization and liberalization released by economic reforms in the wake of 1990s, the Central Public Sector took up the challenge of global competition with great commitment. It had the advantage of the in-built strengths developed in the country during the preceding four decades with unflinching dedication of its human capital. However, the new scenario demanded higher management and technological skills. It is now gearing itself to the new scenario.

The central public sector is wholly committed to deploy advanced technologies to stay competitive and to achieve a long-term sustainability. It is seen as critical to register faster economic and social transformation of India's emerging economy. Innovation and R&D are two important components of growth and performance in today's world of intense global competition.

The Dun & Bradstreet, a leading provider of global business related information, in its report on *India's Top PSUs 2010* pointed out that "R&D expenditure of the 30 PSUs that formed part of this study has been increasing at a higher rate than for private sector companies. Even going back in FY08 and FY09, there has been a clear indication of the emphasis that these companies are laying on R&D." The agency has also found that the private sector has been spending no more than a percent of their profits on R&D.

The trend of R&D spending by the 81 of the operating CPSEs has been shown in Table 1.

Year	R&D Spending Rs crore	PAT Rs crore	R&D Share (%)
1990-91	289.19	2272	12.7
2000-01	849.09	15653	5.4
2005-06	2095.97	69537	3.0
2009-10	2920.22	92593	3.2
2010-11	2444.08	92128	2.65
2011-12	2780.51	97513	2.85

The R&D expenditure as indicated above is more than two-fold of the DSIR data on their recognized inhouse R&D units of CPSEs. The expenditure by them on R&D maintained a near 13% annual growth during the period 1990-91 to 2009-

10. In the last year of reporting 2009-10, there was a near 25% (24.9%) increase in the expenditure over the preceding year.

Hindustan Aeronautics was the largest spender (Rs 832 crore), followed in a close range by BHEL with Rs 829 crore. Bharat Electronics (Rs 316 crore), Indian Oil Corporation (Rs 243 crore), ONGC (Rs 198 crore) and Steel Authority of India (Rs 107 crore) were the major spenders making up for 86.5% of all the spending on R&D. The largest share 61% was claimed by engineering and capital goods segment. Oil and gas has been the other major segment, with a share of over 28% in the total CPS spending in R&D.

Centres of Excellence for Technology Upgradation

The CPSEs, besides establishing dedicated R&D centres have set up centres of excellence for technology upgradation. Predominantly these cover the areas of electric equipment, electricity generation, oil and natural gas, metallurgy, minerals and others. These centres and institutes not only cater to the need for technology upgradation but also are engaged in achieving technology breakthroughs as well. Moreover, the CPSEs have set up institutes, such as in power generation (NTPC) and petroleum (oil CPSEs) for upgradation of personnel skills for leadership role in their respective industries. These institutes have been thrown open to trainees from private sector and from overseas, besides the public sector personnel.

The products manufactured by some of CPSEs are highly technology intensive. Thus, R&D and technology development remain very critical to continuous growth. Intensive in-house efforts have enabled such enterprises to cater to the demands of customers, who are usually well aware of the technological strides made worldwide. This has prompted to continuously scout for new technologies and their acquisition to remain abreast globally of the technological advances. A case in point is of BHEL among others. The CPSE is the first in the world to have developed 80

MVAR Controlled Shunt Reactor to improve power transfer capability of high-voltage transmission systems as a result of its R&D effort.

Participating in Innovation

Many a CPSE besides being directly involved in R&D, are in the forefront of technology upgradation. In the area of electronic warfare simulation, product encryption for communication networks, weather monitoring systems, special nuclear material detection technology including BF_3 detector technology, an established electronics major has been very much involved. It is also actively engaged in tracking celestial sources, besides, research on upgradation in antenna, software for security systems, and several others in defence application electronics.

Gaining Competitiveness through Technology Development

R&D activities in the CPSEs have resulted in the improvement of operational efficiencies in their major techno-economic parameters. SAIL, for example, has succeeded in achieving best ever coke oven consumption at 517/thm, highest-ever productivity of 1.57 t/m^3/day at blast furnaces, highest-ever converter lining life at 11,036 blows in converter at its Bhillai Plant. Besides, SAIL realized highest-ever power generation at 568 MW and the best-ever specific energy consumption of 6.72 gcal/tcs in the year 2009-10.

Product Development

India's oil sector has been in the forefront of technology upgradation. Indian Oil, for instance, has successfully developed more than 180 product formulations at its Research and Development Centre. The CPSE was accorded 65 OEM approvals for its products in the last year. Successful plant trials were carried out at the in-house catalysts developed by the R&D Centre at its refineries at Guwahati, Haldia and CPCL.

Fuel Technologies

The public sector oil companies are collaborating with the National Renewable Energy Laboratory (NREL), USA, in research on alternative fuels. As a result, lifecycle assessment of the use of bio-diesel extracted from Jatropha was operationalised in state transport applications. The efficacy of a modified technology for bioremediation of oil sludge for marine application on oil spillage resulting from a sinking ship, has been successfully demonstrated by a CPSE. The company's R&D Centre was granted 8 patents, including two in the United States, out of 18 patents (including 3 in the United States) during last year. Overall, the CPSE has obtained 215 active patents. Besides, it has 15 MoUs with well-known academic and research institutions for carrying collaborative research activities.

Engineering Breakthroughs for Product Improvements

The R&D Centre of BEML a CPSE is engaged in the design and development of products, critical aggregates, indigenization and other related activities. Over the years, a number of high technology products and equipment for construction and mining, railways and metro, and defence sector through its R&D have been developed by it.

Its launches read out like a roll call of new engineering achievements, such as 125-tonne hydraulic excavator, upgraded version of bulldozer; and transmission and torque convertor. For rail and metro commuting, it launched intermediate cars and maintenance vehicles for metros and aluminium wagons. It developed a snow cutter for defence forces. It also launched a mobile decontamination system, a high mobility truck mounted T-crane and airbrake system for its trucks.

Leveraging Competitive Advances through Technology Development

The key areas of hydrocarbon exploration require seismic data processing, drilling, reservoir management, production technology, ocean engineering, safety and environment protection. R&D institutes catering to basic and applied R&D have been established by the oil CPSE, ONGC. Exploring the latest technologies and striving to overcome the challenges encountered in the exploration and processing industry by evolving alternative routes is the major engagement for these institutes.

The initiatives taken have resulted in several petroleum-related technologies for the development of the Indian E&P sector over the half a century. These have led to critical evaluation of geo-scientific data along with overpressure modelling in and around KG Basin, indicating ample scope for exploration and exploitation of two major unconventional gas systems. As a result of its shale gas desorption study, methodology for HC exploration within basement rocks has been evolved. R&D efforts in biotechnology have led to an improvement in oil production. As a consequence of paraffin control, flow efficiency in flow lines, enhancing oil recovery through microbial system in temperature reservoirs, improving production from stripper wells. Its Institute of Reservoir Studies (IRS) is for instance collaborating to develop selective microbes along with Indian bio-technical institutions (TERI, Delhi; BHU Varanasi; ARI, Pune; and MCRC, Chennai) to develop selective microbes.

The Energy Centre of an oil CPSE is working on biogenic methane from coal and depleted oil reservoirs as collaborative projects with leading research institutions. A project to examine the archived well logs to identify potential uranium rich zones and generate geological models to predict uranium occurrences has been undertaken.

Developing Technologies to Counter Pollutants

Efforts in energy security through dedicated projects by a CPSE have been undertaken. A specific project has two components: development and use of fly ash, and survey and ecological conservation of environment through bioremediation. The entire concern is to explore through R&D, possibilities to put to good use the polluting material discharges. This enables to realize the twin aims of disposal of the pollutants and at the same time to conserve ecological balance in the vicinity of its operational activities.

Fly ash-based pesticides and bio-pesticides have been developed and tested on crops jointly with the Annamalai University. These were also tested in mosquito larvae with Vector Control Research Centre (VCRC), Puducherry. The centre is a dedicated research institution for the study of vector resistance to insecticides, and is also engaged in vector-borne disease control.

These are only a few of the areas in which outstanding results have been secured by the CPSEs. There are many others which have helped them to be more competitive, cost-conscious and enabled them to be more productive.

In MoU between CPSEs and Administrative Ministries five marks have been earmarked for CPSEs efforts towards R&D, Technology Development and Innovation. The guidelines on R&D are also being formulated which would enable PSEs to give further impetus for technology upgradation and innovations. The emphasis should also be on winning patents.

Seeking New Direction

Despite many achievements in science and technology, India is still dependent upon developed countries to import technology. The country needs to build its own capacity, strengthen its technological potency and become self-reliant. It should reduce its dependence on the technology created by the Western world, instead gain competitive edge through its own R&D, technology upgradation and innovation, as well as emerge as a strong nation generating knowledge for growth, for development of the country and for societal transformation.

To realize excellence on the back of scientific platforms, it is essential to broaden the base of science and technology. This can be realized by attracting talented young people and to enrol and train them to become potential scientific leaders. The R&D effort has to focus on advancement of economic and industrial development. Adequate infrastructure for a new era R&D, although developed, needs to be refurbished especially for basic research. This as well calls for infusion of young manpower, which can stimulate innovation and futuristic thinking.

Technology transfer to industry needs to be intensified, while R&D and academic institutions focus on design and product engineering and constantly upgrade the technology desired to be transferred. To that end policies and incentives are needed. Innovation has to be encouraged as a pillar of a national development strategy.

By stimulating government-university-industry collaboration, the task of achieving innovativeness could be better realized. Greater cooperation between industry and the R&D academic institutions for taking advantage of the opportunities is on the upward move. In this process, the public sector plays a significant role. It is incumbent in the present liberalized and competitive environment that more attention is paid to external sources of technology by upgrading existing technology through quantum leaps stimulated by technological inputs.

SKILL DEVELOPMENT (QUESTIONS AND ANSWERS)

Some general questions on Skill Development are answered below:

Q. How important is skill development in India today? Where does India stand?

A. Skill development is interlinked with overall employability. India today doesn't just need employment but better paid employment to drive poverty and build on productivity, innovation and higher growth. Given the 'demographic dividend', India is blessed with the world's youngest workforce that makes the process of skill development crucial in enhancing production possibilities. Therefore, skill development is one area which requires maximum attention by way of internationally benchmarked skill development in a time-bound manner. With such large human resources, India is set to become a super economic power in the world with skilled manpower. Specialization in IT sector has witnessed such an opportunity bringing dominance across the world. On the same pattern, we could develop skill in areas to start a dominant position in other service sectors. Skill development, therefore, is the most essential ingredient of socio-economic growth of our country.

Q. What measures are being taken to facilitate skill development?

A. Let us confess and agree that the education system in India is not evolved enough to give proper space for skill development. A large proportion of Indian labour force is left with outdated skills. As envisaged in the Eleventh Five Year Plan and approach paper to 12th Plan, the formation of a comprehensive national skill development mission through PM's National Council on Skill Development assisted by the National Skill

Development Coordination Board are steps in the right direction. But the requirement is large and infrastructure and facilities are just inadequate.

Q. What role does corporate India play for skill development?

A. The national policy on skill development is an expression of interest and action involving all stakeholders, be it public or private. Corporate India whether public or private, could play the leadership role. But there is urgent requirement for mandatory allocation and yearly target meeting in terms of skill development of working population. Many private and public companies have not only readily acknowledged the serious lacunae in the skill sets of our labour force, but have responded positively by pro-actively setting up of their own training institutions.

Q. What role could central public sector undertakings play?

A. Training and development has always been a distinguishing feature of the CPSUs. The public sector has sought to achieve overall excellence by focusing on good human resource practices and skill development. SCOPE, the apex body of public enterprises has instituted SCOPE Meritorious Award for best practices in Human Resource Management to encourage and reward more PSEs to create opportunities for skill enhancement. The triple bottom-line that the PSEs vouch for in their work processes signifies people, planet and profit. People are the base on which PSEs work to attain meaningful productivity and profitability.

Q. What suggestions do you have to improve upon the present policy on skill development?

A. The challenge is in providing skill development to approximately 500 million people by 2022. There is a need to identify skill development needs of various industry sectors and prepare a catalogue of industry-wise skill types, developing sector skill development plan and skill competency standards. Industrial Training Institutes (ITIs) in every village can restore the relevance of vocational education in the employability of country's youth.

Occupational Safety and Health at Workplace—A Prime Concern

The general index of awareness towards health and safety of working population and the importance of an accident-free industrial environment for upgrading the competitiveness and sustainability of an Enterprise and for national and global economies has risen steadily. Yet, the new world with fading boundaries has a different set of challenges.

We have inherited a highly globalized world, one which is busy finding that elusive foothold between the levels of higher efficiency in productivity (pushed relentlessly by even higher levels of competition) and a disrupted work–life balance. It is evident how the work life has changed, both for the enterprise and the workforce. While the earlier perils of child labour, chemical poisoning, severe fatal accidents are proactively acknowledged and done away with in mind set, legislation and, to a great extent, in implementation, a new set of work-related diseases, most of them psychological and complex in anatomy, have come up.

Occupational Safety and Health (OS&H) in a nutshell, has pronounced moral, legal as well as financial implications and calls for confluence of multiple disciplines involving all stakeholders. An effective OS&H Management and high OS&H performance cannot only scale down the financial responsibilities of an organization by looking to minimize costs related to injuries, stress and stress related illness, medical care bills, sick leave and disability benefits, but also take care of compliance with legal requirements by acknowledging preventive, penalizing and compensatory effect of laws. Thus, it spells a win-win scenario for all

Stakeholders—be it the Government, corporate house or the employees. The Government benefits by increased GNP, corporate houses gain by increased productivity and better image, and the employees get a safe and healthy work environment that boosts their morale and reduces work-related injuries and diseases.

In the last few decades, the paradigm shift in business environment, rapid industrialization and infrastructure development had led to increased activities in manufacturing and construction sector. As a result, complexities of issues and challenges related to occupational safety and health also increased manifold. These include physical, mechanical, biological and chemical hazards. The OH problems are linked to new chemicals and physical hazards, hazards associated with bio technologies and emergence of new occupational diseases of various origins. For example, use of computers in closed buildings lead to "sick building syndrome" which poses new occupational problems. Electromagnetic Fields cause many explored problems, which may surface in future.

As per ILO Report, workers suffer 270 million occupational accidents and 160 million occupational diseases each year - these are conservative estimates. About two million people are killed due to their work every year globally.

Undoubtedly, the hazards at the workplace pose significant risk to property, people and environment. The need of the hour is to adopt successful OS&H practices so that they are adequately examined, and mitigated with strict compliance to statutory requirements.

Legislation on OS&H has existed in India for several decades. Ministry of labour, Government of India and Labour Department of States and Union Territories are responsible for safety and health of workers. The Constitution of India has specified provisions for ensuring OS&H for workers in the form of three Articles i.e. 24, 39 (e & f), and 42. The provisions of OS&H workers as provided in the Constitution are being implemented through the offices of Director General, Mines and Safety (DGMS) and Directorate General Factory Advice

Service and Labour Institute (DGFASLI). DG FASLI provides inputs for national policies on OS&H in Factories and Docks and enforces them through inspectorate of factories and inspectorate of docks while DGMS oversees the health and safety of mine workers and implementation of Mines Act 1952.

Additionally, the National Safety Council (NSC) promotes safety consciousness among workers to prevent accidents, minimize dangers and mitigate human sufferings. NSC is organizing programs, lectures and conferences on safety, conducting educational programs.

In policy and legislation, the government has taken various initiatives to improve OS&H management system within the country to ensure safe and healthy working environments. Announcement of National Policy on Safety Health and Environment is a proactive step with an aim to improve the working conditions and environment at the national level. In order to encourage OS&H and to recognize meritorious performance leading to higher productivity and efficiency the government has instituted Shram Awards, National Safety Awards, Vishwakarma Rashtriya Puraskar and National Safety Award (Mines).

At the international level, International Labour Organization (ILO) has so far adopted 182 conventions and 190 recommendations.

OS&H Management in PSEs

OS&H is an integral part of PSEs' management who employ 14.44 lakh people and about 2 lakh contractual workers. PSEs have well established occupational health techniques, systems and procedures vis-à-vis National Policy on Safety, Health and Environment at Workplace. They have taken effective measures to improve implementation of OS&H in their workplace and follow the best safety practices. Large PSEs have well-defined Safety, Health and Environment policy approved by the Board, which gives direction for various safety, occupational health and environment protection related activities.

In response to the need to continue reducing occupational injuries, illness, fatalities and their associated cost, strategies for augmenting traditional command and control regulatory and management approaches have been explored to further improve performance. Some examples are: behaviour-based safety techniques, improved health and safety risk assessment and auditing methods as well as management system schemes. Further, various approaches such as exercise campaigns and providing exercise facilities and supervised exercised sessions have been used on OS&H to promote employees health.

Overall efforts in occupational health and safety aims to prevent the industrial accidents and diseases and at the same time recognize the relation between the employees' health and safety, the workplace and the environment outside the workplace.

SCOPE, as an apex body of PSEs is playing a catalytic role in strengthening OS&H management System and Practices in PSEs and has formed a "Network of OS&H in CPSEs" under its aegis with collaborative initiative of ILO. It has also been providing a forum to CPSEs in the form of Workshops and Seminars to interact, enhance understanding of the issues on OS&H and evolve appropriate strategy for its implementation at a workplace.

Future Strategy

Occupational Safety and Health is integral to the success of enterprise management. As a result all risks including those arising out of occupational hazards need to be adequately examined and mitigated.

Work process need to be so designed so as to prevent accidents and illness. Existing hazards should be identified and removed from the workplace. The most effective accident and disease prevention begins when work processes are still in the design stage when safe conditions can be built into the work process.

A pro-active approach towards constant medical supervision goes a long way in becoming cost-advantageous as the health of employees as well as employers is always on the surveillance 'radar'. This makes 'prevention' a better tool, helping in early detection, especially in cases where illness is beyond treatment and often irreversible. Hazard related medical examination at workplace needs to be implemented.

Capacity building in OS&H area in industry, Certification of OS&H Professional and Systems, and creating greater awareness about the chemical hazards are essential for maintaining good health of employees. It is essential to emphasize on good lifestyle management including Yogic management Technique for Stress Management.

OS&H related training for effective implementation of OSHMS programmes should be carried out on continuous basis at all levels from top managers to shop floor workers and updated regularly for ensuring knowledge of the system and keep up with changes in the organization. Perfect synchronization between workers' active participation and management's unwavering commitment to health and safety programme is indispensable for a fruitful implementation of Occupational Health and Safety agenda.

Government on its part too can look into constituting an expert committee for review of implementation of thc National policy/Statutory requirements with the participation of Government and Industry Experts. DGFASLI and SCOPE can come together to facilitate this process.

Further, the Government can also consider bringing out an Act for adequate compensation to employees and others affected by disasters, natural or manmade in the lines similar to the scheme existing in USA.

To conclude it can be said that OS&H is a prime area of concern and an essential part of risk management and failure to include it as a key business strategy can have catastrophic results. The aim should be to continually improve towards achieving sustaining healthy and safe working environment.

FINANCIALLY STRESSED PSEs MUST BE REVIVED

To improve is to change; to be perfect is to change often, said Sir Winston Churchill, best known for his leadership of the United Kingdom during the Second World War. Decades have elapsed since then but his words sound true, and business organizations—be in public or private sector—are no exceptions to this dictum. Once blue-chip companies like HMT, ITI and FCI are standing examples of how not changing with the changing times and technologies could change their fate. However, we must accept that there is a silver lining in every dark cloud, and the Standing Conference of Public Enterprises (SCOPE), the apex body of public enterprises, has been advocating for more than two decades the need to revive sick public enterprises to re-vitalize the country's growth engine.

Industrial sickness is not limited to the public sector, in fact commercial enterprises fall sick world over. However, sickness in PSEs has received adverse publicity, affecting the image of the sector. Significantly, many sick companies were taken over from the private sector out of compassion and the social obligation to avoid mass lay-offs. Business also follows Darwin's theory that only the fittest survive. In a demanding and rapidly changing environment, no organization is immune to rough weather. In a liberalized economy, only those shall survive which are ready to change, transform and promote excellence on a daily basis.

The recent introduction of five points under the MoU system is a welcome step but the same should be converted into real applied R&D activities to establish new technologies based on innovation, and not adoption. Care should be taken so that the turnaround is holistic and based on addressing both strategic and operational issues in short and long-terms.

SCOPE's relentless advocacy for reviving the sick units, bore fruit when Prime Minister Manmohan Singh announced that constitution of the Board for Reconstruction of Public Sector Enterprises (BRPSE)—at the conference of Chief Executives of Public Sector Enterprises, organized by SCOPE and DPE (Department of Public Enterprises)—in September 2004. Subsequently, BRPSE, was set up in December 2004 to advise the Government, inter alia, on the measures to restructure/revive, both industrial and non-industrial CPSEs. Since then 67 sick CPSEs have been referred to the BRPSE up to October 2012. The Board has made recommendations in 62 cases while returning five cases to the concerned ministries for further examination. Of the 62 cases, 45 were accepted for revival by the Government while three were closed down. Eighteen of the revived units have already turned around, including Bharat Pumps and Compressors, Cement Corporation of India, HEC, Andrew Yule and MECON, BCCI, National Film Development Corporation, while the others are at various stages of revival.

The Government's recent announcement to revive 11 financially stressed PSEs during 2013-14 is commendable, particularly since the capital infusion in them would be not much for revival but towards writing off interest, penal interest and conversion of loans into equity. In the preceding decade, the number of sick PSEs has come down from 105 in 2002-03 to 63 in 2011-12. If more PSEs turn around, their contribution to the GDP will increase significantly. At present, the CPSEs' contribution to India's GDP ranges between 6% and 7%. This can go up to 10% if loss-making CPSEs start earning profits and profit-making CPSEs continue with their expansion plans.

In 2011-12, profit of 161 profit-making CPSEs increased to Rs.1,25,116 crore compared to Rs.1,13,944 crore by 158 CPSEs in 2010-11, registering a growth of 9.8%. Overall the net profit of all 225 CPSEs stood at Rs.97,513 crore in 2011-12 against Rs.92,128 crore in 2010-11, up by 5.84%.

If you go to find out the reasons for sickness, you will find that both Government and concerned PSEs are equally to blame. Such PSEs did not change with time by changing technology and Government did not clear such projects. Time has come to adopt the change both in letter and spirit.

Since the market situation today is turbulent and cut-throat, prompt attention has to be paid to any sign of sickness from enterprises. A coordinated effort has to be made to deploy signals, benchmarks and road maps to deal with the issue. The MoU system can be made effective in this respect. The BRPSE can also be empowered with greater financial strength by setting aside a part of the disinvestment proceeds for implementing revival plans. Financially better companies, particularly Navratna and Maharatna companies, have a special role to play in the revival of sick units. They could very well examine the possibility of adopting some of the units if not wholly but partially so that they could merge with the mainstream and contribute more in changed circumstances.

PSEs FOR AGRO-BASED ECONOMY

Agriculture is the mainstay of Indian economy. Its development is crucial for the progress of our country and in achieving the goal of inclusive growth. The economic well-being of a majority of our population depends on agriculture as it has direct impact on poverty alleviation, containing inflation, rural incomes and employment generations. Presently, the sector contributes over 14% to national GDP, supports about 2/3rd of our country's population and remains the principal source of livelihood. The sector also has vital supply and demand links with a vast segment of industry.

Hon'ble former President of India, Smt Pratibha Devisingh Patil in her inaugural address in the 2nd Public

Sector Day celebration in Vigyan Bhawan had urged the CPSEs to partner with the agricultural sector and come up with a new viable model of engaging with the farming community and developing rural industry linkages as a part of Corporate Social Responsibility.

Growth and Performance of Agriculture

Since independence, food security of India's growing population has remained the topmost priority of the government. Realization of self-sufficiency in food production led to a major breakthrough in 1960s which transformed the Indian agriculture altogether. The Green Revolution of the 1960s gave birth to a programme on agricultural improvement that brought additional area under cultivation, high yielding seeds, planned irrigation, and adequate protection to agriculture. Successive Five Year Plans laid stress on self-sufficiency and self-reliance in food production. While the Indian planners and policy makers attached great importance to the agriculture sector, the Planning Commission's projection of agriculture sector for the last three decades of achieving 4% growth and contributing to the estimated 10% growth in the economy has not given the desired optimism.

The Eleventh Five Year Plan had targeted Gross Domestic Product (GDP) growth in agriculture and allied activities at 4% per annum. However, GDP Growth in agriculture and allied sector during the first three years of Plan recorded an average growth of 2.03% per annum. In 2007-08, agriculture achieved 5.8% growth but in the consecutive two years, it declined. As per the revised estimates, agriculture (including allied activities) has shown an improved growth of 6.6% as against the estimated growth rate of 5.4% in 2010-11. However, significant measures are needed to accelerate the growth and to achieve the Plan target. For growth to become a reality, necessary support of government and all corporates—public and private, is imperative. All will have to work jointly with farmers of the country to achieve increased production. It may look over-ambitious considering the high number of marginal farmers in India, but it is achievable.

In the Budget for 2010-11, the then Finance Minister Shri Pranab Mukherjee said that he had delineated a four-pronged strategy covering agricultural production, reduction in wastage of produce, credit support to farmers and a thrust to the food processing sector. He said these initiatives have started showing results but there are other issues in the country's food economy that require attention. Acknowledging that the recent spurt in food prices was driven by increase in the prices of items like fruits and vegetables, milk, meat, poultry and fish, which account for more than 70% of the WPI basket for primary food items, he said, removal of production and distribution bottlenecks for these items will be the focus of the government. An allocation under the ongoing Rashtriya Krishi Vikas Yojana (RKVY) was increased from Rs. 6,755 crore in 2010-11 to Rs.7,860 crore in 2011-12.

PSEs Prime Movers of Growth

PSEs are making rich contributions to our country's economic growth as well as to social well-being of its people. PSEs in the agriculture sector have been promoting food security through production of essential inputs in the form of fertilizers, high yield variety seeds, providing food grains to vulnerable section of the population at Central Issue Price (CIP), storage facilities for food grains, in-depth research and production of environment friendly bio-fertilizers. These have been instrumental in contributing their share of responsibility for the agriculture prosperity since their inception. Public Sector Insurance Companies are providing crop insurance and other insurance products related to agriculture to protect the farmers against losses suffered due to crop failure on account of natural calamities. Many PSEs in fertilizer industry have engaged themselves as associates to the Indian farmers in educating, guiding and winning their confidence for proper utilization of fertilizers in the cultivation. While there are over a dozen PSEs directly engaged in agro-based industries, fertilizer production, warehousing activities and public distribution, a large number of them are engaged in rural and infrastructure development on which agriculture prosperity essentially depends.

Emerging Challenges

The country has made great strides towards increasing agricultural production for ensuring food and nutritional security. However, there are still many issues which are impacting the performance and productivity of the sector.

One of the most challenging issues relates to wages of agricultural labour. Asia dominates the regional distribution of the economically active population in agriculture, with about 80% of the world's total agriculture population. Two countries alone, China and India, account for over 60% of the world's agricultural labour force. Millions of these workers earn the lowest wages in the rural sector, lower even than the amount required to subsist. It needs to be taken seriously by government and all the stakeholders in the agriculture sector.

To understand the aspects of rural economy and the important role agriculture labourer plays in that, the sector requires a regulator. The regulator is important, since agricultural labour in India is scattered over 5.6 lakh villages, of which half have a population of less than 500 each. Hence it is difficult to quickly adjudicate agriculture labour issues by labour courts that are already over-burdened. So far, there has been no successful attempt to build an effective organization even at the state level not to speak of the national level. This needs to be corrected at the earliest as possibility of a discontentment amongst the agriculture labour does not augur well for the sector. It will not only hit the government in form of an agitation but eat into the system like a cancer virus.

Fertilizer industry has witnessed significant addition in the fertilizer production capacity. Presently, there are 56 large size fertilizer plants besides 85 medium and small scale units producing SSP. Despite this, the country has to depend upon imports which call for setting up more fertilizer plants to meet the growing requirement of agriculture industry. There is need for review of fertilizer policy to attract investors in this sector.

Huge infrastructure deficit in rural India has affected the pace of overall economic development and agricultural production. Government as well as corporate sector needs to pay attention on the development of rural and agriculture infrastructure on priority basis. Connectivity, a key factor of rapid rural transformation, ensures an effective and efficient agricultural marketing system.

Our agricultural marketing system suffers from problems of: inadequate number of organized markets; inadequate progress of cooperative marketing; lack of adequate rural godowns, warehouses and cold storage facilities; poor market and price information system, weak integration of production system with post-harvest value chains resulting in high cost of marketing and low price realization by farmers; lack of quality consciousness, grading, standardization, etc.

Adequate water availability for irrigation is another important factor for enhancing crop productivity. There is need for implementation of efficient Water Management System for proper utilization of water in low rainfall areas and taking care of problem of soil erosion and good drainage system in most heavy rainfall areas. Uncontrolled construction of flats by builders on agricultural land should be checked to maintain and increase agricultural produce. Enhanced investments, gender issues and capacity building of farmers are some other issues that need to be addressed urgently to improve competitiveness of Indian agriculture.

To begin with, successful studies and research undertaken by National Seeds Corporation (NSC) can be better utilized. There are seed varieties developed by NSC that can withstand any drought, rice varieties that can grow and survive floods, fruits and vegetable seeds that have high yield and lower growth cycles. To make them available to farmers, a better marketing system and a better seed distribution arrangement is needed. A number of PSEs have rural reach which can be converted into distribution points.

An important area that can save more than 45% of the wastage in fruits and vegetable is the transport from farm to the vegetable market. This is an area that could be taken up as a priority by the public sector companies including railways. Public sector companies need to develop close interaction with institutes like Indian Council of Agricultural Research (ICAR) to develop demand-driven technologies for benefit of small farmers and other marginalized social groups. The effort could boost the growth of agri-entrepreneurs that government has been trying to promote.

There is no magic wand that can resolve the issues in agriculture. However, global efforts taken by the international organizations like Food and Agricultural Organization (FAO) to strengthen agriculture and allied activities can be replicated in India. The decision taken either regarding the agriculture labour or the farming techniques can be shared. The opportunities are plenty.

PSEs ARE NOT EXCITED ABOUT SHARE BUYBACK PROPOSAL

Government's plan to raise Rs.40,000 crore in the current fiscal year by divesting a part of its shares in the Central Public Sector Enterprises (CPSEs) through public offers has run aground. Now the Government has mooted the idea of CPSEs buying back the shares from Government, in a change of disinvestment strategy to raise funds.

Some of the unanswered questions on Buyback proposal are as follows:

Q. Do you see any possibility that the Government would raise a decent amount through the disinvestment route?

A. Almost every year, the Government has been fixing a target for disinvestment in PSEs. For 2010-11, the Government had set a target of Rs.40,000 crore, but could mop only Rs.22,762.96 crore despite comparatively better market conditions. This year, i.e. in 2011-12, the Government again had set a target of Rs.40,000 crore, and so far only Rs.1,144.55 crore has been raised.

With just three months left in this financial year, the target is unlikely to be met, as the market has been volatile and uncertain. Since the stock markets cannot be trusted to give good returns, the investors' sentiments are at an all-time low.

Cash Rich PSEs and Budget Deficit PSEs are not really excited about the proposal as they have their own plans of expansions and acquisitions. In the backdrop of a global slowdown, these PSEs feel that it would be difficult for them to raise financial resources from the market for funding their capital expenditure plans. Internal resources and cash surplus must be left for expansion plan of PSEs.

Q. What are the PSEs' reservations about the share buyback proposal?

A. Most of the Central PSEs are competing in the global market. They have elaborate plans of investments. The power sector PSEs are gearing up to add about 1,00,000 MW during the 12th Five Year Plan (2012-17). The investment in the sector is pegged at Rs.13.72 lakh crore. Coal India is keen to employ its reserve cash to expand its production, and acquire companies and mines overseas. It plans to invest about Rs.30,000 crore in the 12th Five Year Plan, i.e. Rs.6,000 crore annually from FY 2013-17.

In the case of manufacturing PSEs, their cash surpluses are not large in relation to their investment plans while a company like Power Grid needs the cash for expanding its infrastructure of transmission capacities. Oil and gas companies also have the requirement of huge capital for exploration, production and infrastructure.

Cash reserves serve as a buffer for companies during tough market conditions. It would not be prudent for the government to strip PSEs of their cash reserves.

Q. How will it affect the investor sentiments?

A. Any proposal should be investor friendly. The share buy-back scheme could adversely impact investor sentiments at a time when the stock markets are already depressed. It is important to safeguard the interest of small investors. Already, in India, we are far away from developing confidence of individual equity holders, so much so in U.S. whereas 43% personal saving of individual is invested in equity whereas in India it must be less than 1%.

Q. How does the proposal get with corporate governance principles?

A. The proposed scheme raises serious concerns in the area of corporate governance, as the decision about what to do with their cash holdings should be left solely to the Boards of public enterprises. They may desire to buy some businesses or expand into related businesses or make portfolio investments, and it is not difficult to see that their decisions would be completely different from those of the Government. In effect, this proposition undermines the capabilities and authority of the Board of Directors who are competent enough to take such decisions after considering relevant factors, which may be different for each PSE.

Q. What are the credible options that the Government can consider?

A. An option that Government may consider whether there can be cross-holding, i.e. PSEs buying one another's shares. This was attempted first time in 1998-99 when three oil sector enterprises, i.e. GAIL, ONGC and IOC mopped up about Rs.5,000 crore. Over the years, above cross-holdings have proved to be profitable, showing that equity investment by PSEs in each other generates value over a period. Cross-holding is a better route than share buyback for the disinvestment of Government's stakes in PSEs.

MANDATORY LISTING OF PSEs

PSEs in India represent a class of superb, system-oriented corporate entities. Any mandatory listing may adversely affect their credibility, market standing and autonomy. PSEs don't shy away from meeting listing norms, but doing so requires appropriate timing and it should be left to respective Boards to decide the time frame, amount and valuation, depending on market conditions.

PSEs in India were established on the twin premise of economic development and social justice. A post-independence agrarian-based economy required a shift to an industry-based economy. Profit was not the only objective and PSEs were more concerned with socio-economic issues so the result was comparatively lower profit. Post-liberalization, reforms in PSEs provided a solid foundation, as a result of which PSEs have been branded the creator of wealth for the nation. The period 1990 to 2010 saw a phenomenal increase in the all-round development of PSEs, whether it was an almost 10 times increase in turnover, a 35 times increase in net profit and sustained positive growth even during the economic meltdown. This is why Indian PSEs became a role model for the world during the recession. Today, PSEs account for one-third of the Government's revenue, about 1% of over 4,000 companies listed on the market and 25% of the market capitalization.

One of the considerations for mandatory listing is that corporations manipulate the market from time to time and there was a need for regulatory and ethical norms. It would be worth mentioning that PSEs can't and should not be placed in the same bracket as large corporations since PSEs do not play the market. There are a large number of checks and balances together with mandatory provisions such as internal and external audit systems, Board Audit Committees, the Comptroller and Auditor General (CAG) and disclosures norms for board-level positions that keep PSEs away from unethical dealings and market manipulation. There is a proper transparent annual accounting system and, above all, the Central Vigilance Commission guards the guardians in PSEs.

The post-liberalization listing of PSEs has brought out hidden worth. As of now, a little over 50 PSEs (including banks) have been listed, of which 25 to 30 have a public float of less than 25%. Listing to such a level would require about Rs.1,25,000 crore. If all the PSEs are taken into consideration, listing to that level may require over Rs.3,80,000 crore. The next question that arises is: where is the appetite? Flooding the market with many offerings will subdue the capital market and the real worth of the PSEs in such cases may not come out. Listing some of the best PSEs in the recent past gave such an indication and, therefore, PSEs should not, need not and cannot be put under a time-bound mandatory listing, whether it is 25% or even 10%.

One of the other considerations given in favour of listing is the accountability factor for large many shareholders. This logic probably does not hold good for PSEs because, being government-held, they are also accountable to the people at large because Government is of, for and by the people. PSEs are the custodian of public money and, therefore, are accountable to the public and are responsible to Parliament through its Committee on Public Undertakings (COPU). PSEs are accessible through the "Right to Information" (RTI) law and, therefore, represent an altogether different class in the corporate sector. All these indicate that PSEs can't be put in the same basket with other corporations.

Therefore, mandatory listing would not be appropriate for PSEs and if such provision is required for PSEs, it would be best to consider a 10% employee stock option (ESOP) and incentivize it to solve the issue of attrition and improve employees' sense of belonging.

REFORM NEEDED IN R&D SECTOR

It is not difficult to apply your mind and think out of the box for better results. On the funny side, just like, in the Bollywood movie "Three idiots" the boys used vacuum cleaners for sucking baby from womb!

After all what is innovation and research? It is probably the outcome of necessity, combined with frustration and urge to find out the remedies? It does not necessarily always happen in laboratories of repute. Newton never sat in a laboratory to innovate that there is a gravitation force! It requires dedication and thinking. There is no doubt that today students are not exposed to research and practical ways of learning that from early age would give them an opportunity to create. There is no career path for innovation because there is lots of pressure to choose a stable career somewhere else. Therefore, school and college education level must imbibe the scientific spirit in our children instead of the emphasis on the system of homework and rote learning.

In spite of an all-time emphasis on it, unfortunately, R&D has become just an ivory tower today for chanting a mantra from the top, giving best speeches, arranging visit of dignitaries to R&D labs and of course taking large benefits of tax-discounts. The result is that even after so many decades, we still depend upon import of technology and look outside even to smaller countries. Obviously there is something wrong somewhere and R&D today requires relook and reform in our country.

The first step would be conducting total audit of R&D expenditures through independent auditors and evaluate them with respect to technology developed. All ritualistic approach on R&D should be taken away. Institutionalized and sector-wise R&D with dedicated R&D efforts need to be taken in the field of technology, healthcare and medicine, management and energy etc. Adoption of technology should be discouraged, instead, indigenous technological advancement be made for self-reliance. Intellectual right protection and incentivized regulation should be introduced. Law enforcement agencies, scientists, corporates, ministries and general public must be educated to change the mind-set towards innovation and research.

It is unfortunate that industry has not converted the incentives given by Government for becoming self-reliant in technology, be it public or private sector. Large many statistics with expenditures and number of laboratories set-up have remained only for the purpose of good show in documentation centres. A significant growth of R&D Centres for the purpose of taking financial benefits should be curbed. Application of shop floor research must be tested at pilot plant level to convert them to commercial plants.

Disinvestment of PSEs will provide good opportunity to utilize the part of proceeds for development of R&D. Sector-wise innovation and R&D through institutionalization would give better results. Corporates, both public and private must allocate certain percentage of their profit for R&D. A mandatory provision to this effect combined with audit and feedback mechanism for evaluation of R&D centres would yield better results.

PRODUCTIVITY AND INNOVATION – MUST FOR EMERGING ECONOMY

Productivity is synonym with competitiveness. Its growth is seen as a major indicator of economic progress and improvement in quality of life. In the corporate world today, the drivers of productivity and competitiveness are increasingly giving equal importance to efficiency and quality, innovation and entrepreneurship.

Manufacturing is crucial to our economy. India has potential to emerge as major manufacturing hubs for the global market. This can materialize only with the improvement in competitiveness of its industry. Rising productivity is the key to manufacturing and improving competitiveness of the same.

Challenges

Today, Economic Recession is being experienced by most of the economies world over. The impact of slowing output and the apparent fall in demand and labour productivity is a cause of alarm. It has been observed that the productivity growth in many advanced economies fell by more than half in 2011 compared to 2010. Though there is a measure of relief when we observe productivity growth rates to remain comparatively higher in emerging economies, nevertheless, the average global productivity growth seems headed for a downward trend if innovation does not step up to arrest this fall.

Some Global Facts

Global Gross Domestic Product (adjusted for inflation) fell from 5% in 2010 to 3.9% in 2011; average employment growth remained unchanged when compared to the previous year (at 1.4%). In 2011, global labour productivity growth (average change in output per person employed) fell to 2.5% from 3.6% in 2010. These facts show that less output growth was a result of falling productivity. It has been projected that the average global productivity growth will fall from 2.5 in 2011 to 2.3 in 2012 if recession stays on. The main reasons are: falling output in advanced economies like US, Europe and Japan. In the Euro Area, sovereign debt and bank crisis dampened the growth in output, while in Japan a natural disaster like 'tsunami' hindered healthy growth in output.

In emerging economies, like India, Brazil, China and Mexico, though employment growth has also registered a marginal fall even though globally these emerging economies are the most important job creators, the overall fall in output growth clearly points to a decline in productivity. Here it is important to note that employment generation is facing threats in the form of demographic impact of lower birth rates. Average employment growth in emerging and developing economies was 1.6% in 2010 and reached only 1.5% and is projected to be even lower.

Total Factor Productivity (TFP) which is a measure of the efficiency of production and is measured as output per person employed has slowed down from 1% in early 2000s to around 0.5% currently. A slowdown in TFP growth mirrors a slowdown in technological progress and innovation. In US, TFP is on a downward trend post-recession. While in the Euro Area, the TFP has shown dismal performance for as long as thc past decade. In both these advanced economies, a falling TFP points out to a weakening capacity for innovation. Transitional growth eventually erodes and the combined effect of large investment and fewer reforms in these emerging economies creates areas for declining marginal returns and less productivity from those investments. However, the shift of economic activity from advanced to emerging economies favours countries with higher productivity growth rates.

Causes of Concern

Prime Minister Dr. Manmohan Singh while addressing the Chief Executives of Public Enterprises on the occasion of presentation of SCOPE Excellence Awards and MoU Awards held on 31st January 2012 emphasized the need to perform better in manufacturing. "We must increase the share of the manufacturing sector in our GDP from the present unsatisfactory level of 15%. The Central Public Sector Enterprises have a significant presence in areas such as machine tools, heavy transport, earth moving and mining equipment, ship building, defence equipment, aerospace, heavy electrical equipment and nuclear power generation" he said urging CPSEs in these areas to embark upon ambitious plans of expansion to make the target of 12-14% growth in the manufacturing sector a living reality.

Earlier, Principal Scientific Advisor to the Government of India, Dr. P Chidambaram while delivering SCOPE Lecture on Research, Innovation and Sustainable Development in May 2011 had said, "The Future growth of our country, I think, will be driven by manufacturing sector. In the 2010 Global Manufacturing Competitiveness Index, Deloitte and the US Council on Competitiveness ranked India second after China with the note that "India is gaining an even stronger foothold on that position over the next five years" (Deloitte 2010).

Knowledge, Innovation and Manufacturing – Drivers of Progress

Alvin Toffler of National Academy of USA said in early seventies 'Yesterday' people dominated through violence, 'today' they dominate through the capital and 'tomorrow' the domination will be through knowledge. Winton Churchill once said, *"The future rulers shall be the owners of knowledge"*. This 'TOMORROW' has become today. The world is moving fast into the knowledge and innovation economy. Innovation has been and is the major driver of progress playing pivotal roles in economics, business intelligence, strategic planning and technology.

In the developing countries particularly the GDP growth rate is dependent more on innovation capacity. Innovation thrives in a competitive environment. It generates economic value, new jobs in the economy and cultures of entrepreneurship, thus promotes productivity and economic growth. But if the growth rate is to be sustained over a long period there is need to lay a strong foundation for basic research besides retraining and developing its innovation capacity. For this reason, a country generally must have both the programme of research in all its dimensions and a set of supports for innovation against in all its dimensions—product innovation, process innovation and design innovation. However, in India, in spite of favourable policies and allocations, the technological development has not been to the desired level. India's dependency on developed countries in terms of importing technology is a matter of concern. It needs to build its own capacity, strengthen its technological potency and become self-reliant.

Prime Minister Dr Manmohan Singh in his inaugural address at the 98th Indian Science Congress held in January 2011 declared the present decade as the "Decade of Innovation" and the year 2012-13 as the 'Year of Science'. The focus therefore would be on basic research and innovation. The Prime Minister also approved the establishment of a National Innovation Council to draw a roadmap for the decade of innovation.

In manufacturing, technological innovation comes in two forms. First, new inventions provide a leap forward in technology. The other form of innovation comes from the steady improvement in products and manufacturing processes within major technology life cycles. Both major and incremental innovations are necessary and need encouragement.

Productivity in Public Enterprises

In the early 1960s, PSEs adopted the productivity concepts partnering with the National Productivity Council (NPC). The Bureau of Public Enterprises (BPE) – now called Department of Public Enterprises – made the PSEs adopt techniques of better management of inputs, harnessing equipment and material resources through enhanced utilization of installed capacities. PSEs focused on technology, R&D and innovation including quality improvement initiatives, energy conservation, besides budgetary and cost controls. The efforts also centred on performance improvement by effective management systems that foster employee involvement and motivation thus building a progressive management culture with human face. The outcome of which is that the trained public sector executives have become an attractive talent source for the private sector.

Productivity Enhancement Techniques Adopted by PSEs

Some of the holistic approaches that are effectively adopted for productivity enhancement in the current turbulent global business world are: (i) self-assessment; (ii) Bench-marking; (iii) Integrated Management Systems; (iv) Quality Management like ISO-9000, 14000; (v) Business Process Re-engineering; (vi) Balanced Scorecard; (vii) Six Sigma; (viii) Supply Chain Management and (ix) Enterprise Resource Planning (ERP). Most of these techniques rely on human involvement, innovation and creativity.

PSEs have not lagged behind in adopting tools of productivity enhancement which have also enabled them to adopt Total Quality Management (TQM), Human Resource Development (HRD), Talent Management Systems, Customer Relationship Management (CRM). They have, thus not only kept pace with the innovative management, but have often gone ahead in adapting and adopting modern tools and techniques to its operative systems competing with the private corporates.

Steps Taken for Performance Improvement in PSEs

Some of the measures taken by the Government and the management of CPSEs to improve the performance of public enterprises are as under:

- Strengthening of MoU System
- Periodic performance review by the Administrative Ministries and Inter Ministerial Committee
- Delegation of enhanced powers to the Board of Directors of Maharatna, Navratna and Miniratna CPSEs and other profit making PSEs
- Professionalization of Board of Directors and induction of eminent persons as Independent Directors
- Setting up of Board for Reconstruction of Public Sector Enterprises (BRPSE) to consider inter alia revival/ restructuring of sick and loss making CPSEs
- Training and human resource development
- Cost controls
- Diversification of product mix
- Technology upgradation, research and development
- Better housekeeping and improved maintenance management practices
- Greater emphasis on energy conservation
- Improved inventory control
- Export promotion

In spite of the above measures, there remain some issues for effective good governance and to sustain growth momentous amidst rising competition. These include separation of ownership and Board level management, succession planning, operational autonomy and Board reforms, overload of Independent Directors and their evaluation, etc.

Growth of Labour and Capital Productivity in CPSEs

The Indian Central public sector witnessed an increase in labour as well as capital productivity during the two decades since the ushering in of the economic reforms. Labour productivity, calculated as gross value added divided by number of people employed, increased by a multiple of 6 in the decade 1990-2000 and by a higher multiple of 18 during 1990-2010.

Table I

Growth of Labour and Capital Productivity in CPSEs

Year	Productivity		Productivity Index	
	Labour (Rs lakh)	Capital (Ratio)	Labour	Capital
1990-91	1.44	0.24	100	100
2000-01	8.76	0.43	608	179
2009-10	26.30	0.36	1826	150

Capital productivity measured as gross value addition divided by capital employed which incorporates net worth and long-term loans registered an increase from 0.24 in 1990-91 to 0.36 by the end of 2009-10. However, there is a fall in capital productivity in the last decade, 2000 to 2010, which is explained by a relatively larger expansion in net worth.

Department of Public Enterprises, Ministry of HI&PE, Government of India measures productivity of CPSEs by using some of the important parameters of capacity utilization, inventory in relation to sales energy used in public enterprises.

The Capacity utilization in CPSEs during 2009-10 has been better than previous years. As many as 50 CPSEs out of a sample of 75 units recorded capacity utilization of 75% and more during 2009-10 as compared to 43 CPSEs out of 74 units in 2008-09 and 48 CPSEs out of 77 units in 2007-08. The Table II below indicates capacity utilization in CPSEs during the last three years.

Table - II

Capacity Utilization in PSEs

S.No	Description	2009-10	2008-09	2007-08
1.	Units which have recorded 75% or more capacity utilization	50(67)	43(58)	48(62)
2.	Units which have recorded 50% or more but less than 75%	10(13)	15(20)	16(21)
3.	Units which have recorded less than 50% capacity utilization	15(20)	16(22)	13(17)
	Total	**75(100)**	**74(100)**	**77(100)**

Figures shown in brackets show percentage
Source: Public Enterprises Survey 2009-10

The Asian Productivity Organization (APO) evolved a new concept of productivity called Green Productivity (GP). It is concerned with the last two elements of the Triple Bottom-line, i.e. People and Planet which talks about environmental protection and social fairness. CPSEs are figured among the top companies to get certification for the ISO standards, be it 14000 for environment, 22000 for CSR, Global Compact of UN and others.

There are numerous human resource management (HRM) policies initiated by PSEs. These include talent management through proper training programmes; job rotation; competitive compensation and reward systems; competency mapping; succession planning; retirement, post-retirement, voluntary retirement scheme (VRS) policies; career path planning; caring for the welfare of employees and their families. For skill development, CPSEs have promoted intensively on-the-job training, in-house training programmes and external training programmes for their employees. Many CPSEs have set up educational institutes for imparting training like the Power Management Institute in Noida set up by NTPC.

Way Forward

India's growth in recent times has been driven by the services and the manufacturing sector. India enjoys significant advantages in these areas, through its availability of skilled manpower, lower costs and a large and growing domestic market. However, for a long term sustained growth the low cost advantage is not enough. Research has shown that the Indian manufacturing sector has advantage of high value added manufacturing as compared to China, which is predominantly into high volume and low technology manufacturing. This differentiation helps to gain competitive advantage.

However, India needs to broaden its base of science and technology. This can be realized by attracting talented young people and to enrol and train them to become potential scientific leaders. Technology transfer to industry also needs to be intensified while R&D and academic institutions focus on design and product engineering and constantly upgrade the technology desired to be transferred. To this end, policies and incentives are needed from the government. There is also need to develop programmes to nurture industry-academia collaborations and encourage Indian scientists to work on problems important to India's future as well as on those of global significance. Building networks to connect academia and industry are required to be facilitated.

Indian Public Sector has been productivity conscious, be it labour productivity, capital productivity, total factor productivity or green productivity. CPSEs also put emphasis on labour management cooperation and worker participation as a more practical approach to incentivize work and to increase retention of employees. They have adopted good Corporate Governance Practices and are pace setters in fulfilling their social responsibilities. It is because of these they have not been affected to the extent other corporates in India and world over during the recession. The need is that all corporates should not only make the best use of factors contributing towards productivity but also adopt ethical practices, promote concepts of people management and ecological balance.

CONSULTANCY SERVICES IN PSEs

Consulting, by definition, is to provide professional counsel to an individual or organization for a fee. The nature of service rendered can be purely advisory or a combination of well researched selective guidance followed by implementation of solutions recommended. The content of service thus provided is a mix of a certain degree of analysis, measurement or testing, sample testing; data processing services and inference thus drawn upon which the expert advice is based and the execution/application of the same is based. Hence, Consulting, by all measures, is a matter elevated beyond the confines of domain knowledge, seeking highly localized and selective expertise and solutions varying from case to case, crucially dependent on a high degree of intellectual input, often falling outside the purview of a certain enterprise or industry. For example, while manufacturing industry may have an appropriate understanding of the industries with which it shares forward and backward linkages, it may be left grappling in the dark when it comes to management, financial or information technology related issues.

How have consultancies made their way into the main-stream business models? Myriad reasons may push organizations to engage a consulting team. Simple transaction-cost economics opines that a task out of routine and done least in an organization would incur more cost than passing it on to experts. Besides paucity of time, the cushioned security net an 'expertise' or 'expert opinion' grants to bolster the image of decision making processes in an organization is an added advantage. Also, there is an undefined, underlying need to validate and verify such decision making or brainstorming. Added legal liability that consultants provide against any decision gone wrong is a win-win situation for the clients.

The need to augment core manufacturing industry by detailed and meticulous, localized solutions, be it managerial or technical, makes good business sense. Finally, government as an agency, both as a client and a legislator is conspicuous. For example, a government may prevent banks from engaging in non-banking activities and hence provide a significant push to consultants to supplement banks' non-banking activities. Good governance is bad politics, but good business. Across the globe, the indispensability of engaging consultants as a major tool to revamp and break down the complex bureaucratic redundancies and increase productivity and efficiency is adequately noted. Private consultants are being trusted with strategic solutions to operational challenges. In US, where the consulting industry found its first solid foothold, followed by UK, fostering efficiency with division of labour by hiring consultants for specialized jobs is tried and tested. Internationally, names like McKinsey & Company (Management consulting), Booz

& Company (Management Consulting), Deloitte (Financial Consulting), Ernst & Young (Accounting), Accenture (Management Consulting), PricewaterhouseCoopers (Accounting), etc., have helped governments execute massive makeovers of projects. For example, in UK, McKinsey and Company has played an important role in sectors like infrastructure and railways. In USA similarly, McKinsey & Company handled the transformation envisioned by North Carolina's Department Of Transport. In Germany, Booz is credited with reorganizing Public Sector Pension Plan. It is interesting to note that Public sector is emerging as the prime market for private consultants. Kennedy Information, an American firm that monitors global consulting industry, stipulated that globally, public sector accounts for about 30% of the consulting market. In India, the story so far is of a parallel trend—while government is increasingly depending on private consultancies to streamline their work-processes in order to increase efficiency and cut down on costs, a network of public sector consultancies are already providing the economy with strong foundation of numerous consultancies.

An example of the influence of private consultants on governance is that of the e-governance portal of Andhra Pradesh, covering services for issuance of birth and marriage certificates, tax information, vehicle registration, land registration, pension and bill payments, etc., being handled by TCS, built and operated by it, for the state's population of around 75 million citizens. This follows from the fact that it is very costly and impractical for governments to upgrade department's IT systems. It has been argued that consultancies reap certain benefits for the government by way of ensuring stepping up of the technological matrix of the government agencies. They work their expertise by building up certain sets of applications which can be applied with ease for resolving issues which are severely time bound. They also help strengthen government institutions politically by helping them build an image of a modern organization which considers technological advancement as a key to increasing efficiency.

A number of consultancies, under the aegis of different ministries are working towards this purpose too. In India, consultancy has been viewed as a private sector prerogative as, by nature, private sector is more competitive and desirous of adoption of 'best practices'. While public sector may not have been the breeding ground for such consultancies, they have slowly matured and come out of the niche of core manufacturing industries to expand into the consultancy/ services sector. The public sector plunged deep into building the core competencies of our economy post-independence; the practice of seeking expert services started gaining ground with growth in number of consultants.

Public sector so far, boasts some of the stalwarts in the game. For example, Engineers India Limited (EIL), which was established in 1965, provides engineering and related technical services for petroleum refineries and other industrial projects. EIL works under the administrative control of Ministry of Petroleum and Natural Gas (MoP&NG), Government of India. It also caters to India's design, engineering and turnkey contracting requirements, providing a complete range of project services needed to conceptualize, plan, design, engineer and construct projects to meet the specific requirements of its clients.

Telecommunications Consultants India Ltd. is another PSE under Ministry of Communications and Information Technology Dept. of Telecommunications. TCIL was set up in 1978 for providing Indian telecom expertise in all fields of telecom, Civil and IT. The company majors in fields of Switching, Transmission Systems, Cellular services, Rural Telecommunication, Optical fiber based backbone transmission systems, IT & Networking Solutions, Application Software, e-Governance, 3G Network, WIMAX Technology and also Civil construction projects.

EdCIL (Education Consultants India Ltd.) is another public sector organization established in 1981 under Ministry of Human Resource Development Dept. of Secondary Education and Higher Education and offers consultancy and technical services in different areas of Education and Human Resource Development. It caters to domestic as well as international clients. Other examples are of MECON Limited, Water and Power Consultancy, etc.

Another pioneering concept is establishment of Consultancy Development Center, which is an independent organization of Department of Scientific and Industrial Research (DSIR), Ministry of Science and Technology, Government of India set up for promotion, development and strengthening of consultancy skills and capabilities in the country including enhancement of export of consultancy and professional services. It takes its services across the border to countries like Kazakhstan, Morocco, Israel and Turkey, discovering new talents and strengthening consultancy skills. Water and Power Consultancy are also doing good and earning foreign exchange as well.

According to the Economic Survey (2011-2012), the volume of revenue in the Indian consulting industry on conservative basis has been estimated at around US$ 8.24 billion in 2010-11. Presently, it contributes to about 0.47% of the GDP which is not commendable as compared to many countries.

Currently, about 7,000 consultancies are in operation across metropolitans like Delhi, Bangalore, Hyderabad, Chennai, Mumbai, Pune and Kolkata. Countries which have acknowledged the strong presence and competitive advantage of India in consultancy business are US, UK, Japan, China and more recently, the European Union. The other countries that are looking for Indian consultancy firms to provide them innovative ways for projects execution also include Vietnam, in the field of textile and garments, energy, geology and mining, agriculture, rural development, transportation and tourism. The mainstay of Indian consultancy organizations are, professional having competence in structure, civil engineering, telecommunications, power, chemical, petrochemicals, and computer software are the strong areas of Indian consultancies. Main functionalities are market studies, system designing, feasibility and erection and commissioning of plant and machinery.

However the industry is also beset with challenges. Increased networking opportunities need to be harnessed to guarantee higher levels of standardization, boosting consultancies. Low quality assurance, scant overseas presence due to lack of intensified market intelligence, etc., need to be adequately addressed. The prime objective of setting up consultancies in India was the need to provide self-reliance in technology, including designing, detailing and supervision cum commissioning of projects. Somewhere along the line though, the objective seems lost in the complex jargon of government policy, ill implemented, ill-timed and lack of planning initiative. Also, the consultancies need R&D centres as their workshops and lack of such integrated R&D centres belies the whole point behind these consultancies. Without these research centres which complement the whole process of knowledge building and innovation, consultancies remain skeletal. In spite of a good network of consultancies India has, ironically, been borrowing and even buying technology from other smaller economies. Another grey area is the need for policy initiatives to protect the domestic and indigenous technology innovations.

Thus, consultancies have proven to assist greatly in improving service delivery and cut down costs, thereby increasing public spending. They also boost the governments' ability to deliver public services. The expertise the consultants provide is a result of the evolving needs of markets it serves, more and more technologically advanced, so much so that it requires special, separate and totally focused efforts to plug the gap. We need to monitor the transformational effect of these consultancies.

STATE LEVEL PUBLIC SECTOR ENTERPRISES IN BAD SHAPE

State Level Public Enterprises (SLPEs) form a dominant part of State economy and play a very important role in the overall development. These are the 'corporations' (set up by Acts of the State Legislatures) or 'Companies' (set up with approval of State Governments). They also act as an instrument to operationalize the central schemes in some of the States. Though SLPEs are extended arms of the State Governments in the task of the promotion of economic and social development, the current difficult economic situation of the country, calls on them to take onerous responsibility for boosting the growth of the economy. The broad Vision and Aspiration which the Twelfth Plan seeks to fulfil is "Faster, Sustainable and More Inclusive Growth' that demands significant contribution from the States.

Many States have resolved to achieve growth rates in State Domestic Product (SDP) in their respective States/ UTs close to or higher than the all India target growth rate of 8.2% for the 12th Plan. To achieve the objectives of growth, investment and productivity are the two essential requirements. SLPEs are the vehicle of such investment as well as for enhancing the productivity in the States. A huge amount of investment and manpower resources have been invested in them. The total number of people employed in these State Enterprises exceeds even those in Central Public Sector Enterprises (CPSEs).

The National Survey on State Level Public Enterprises 2008-09 and 2009-10, published by Department of Public Enterprises (DPE) dwells on the performance of SLPEs. Out of the 863 operating State Level Public Enterprises (SLPEs), only 624 enterprises furnished information on the performance of their respective SLPEs. As per the Survey, 384 SLPEs earned profits, as many as 215 SLPEs incurred losses during 2009-10 and 25 SLPEs reported no profit/loss. While CPSEs in the year 2011-12 with total investment of Rs.7.29 lakh crore, contributed total turnover of over Rs. 18 lakh crore, these 624 reporting SLPEs, have a total investment of Rs 5,18,209 crore and total turnover of Rs 3,66,814 crore. In case of CPSEs, the ratio of turnover to GDP for the year 2011-12 was 22% as against 6% in case of SLPEs.

The overall net loss at the aggregate level for the 624 SLPEs in 2009-10 stood at Rs (-) 13,227 crore as against an aggregate loss of Rs (-) 17,866 crore for 614 SLPEs in 2008-09, showing a decrease of 25.96% in aggregate losses during 2009-10 over 2008-09. SLPEs generated a negative rate of return on investment which was (-) 3.03% in 2009-10 against CPSEs positive return on investment at over 18% in 2011-12.

Top slots among the top Ten States in terms of Losses by SLPEs goes to Uttar Pradesh (23.57%); Delhi (16.82%); Punjab (6.86%); Haryana (4.96%); Rajasthan (3.01%); Jammu and Kashmir (2.37%); Tamil Nadu (1.92%); West Bengal (1.75%); Andhra Pradesh (1.30%); and Bihar (1.05%).

It is evident from the above that SLPEs are not in good shape and there is need to strengthen them through restructuring, technological upgradation and effective management.

Dr. Manmohan Singh while speaking at Annual CEO's Conference of CPSEs observed:

"There are hundreds of SLPEs with vast sums of public money invested in them. They must also change and adapt to the needs of the times. Given the state of State Government finances, many State Governments are unable to afford luxury of large number of loss-making enterprises. We must therefore find viable means to revive and sustain such enterprises and ensure that interests of workers and employees are not hurt due to political interference and bad management".

SLPEs are in bad shape no doubt but what is the cause of their pathetic condition and an examination of the same indicates that they are highly politicized and most of them have political Chairpersons who are appointed by State Government for extraneous reasons. Such political Chairpersons come with fixed agenda and do not provide vision for growth of the enterprise. They also have big gap with the management who are responsible for strategy and its implementation. State Governments are also responsible for not paying adequate attention to these enterprises and leave them in the lurch and dilapidated conditions. There is no professionalization in state enterprises and industrial relation is very poor; quite often employees go on strike. There is a complete lack of belongingness and any initiative to motivate them. Shortage of resources, exposure to the outer world of business, overstaffing are the other reasons. Working with work centres is secondary as many of them prefer to be outside which affects the business output. Consequently, state enterprises have rather become liabilities than assets and with a passage of time a sizeable number have become extinct (like dinosaur).

What is the remedy therefore? It seems that there is need for radical reform in terms of the thinking process of the State Governments, professionalization, training, working against targets, and evaluation by the concerned state ministry through "Quarterly Performance Review" (QPR) meetings conducted by the Secretary of the department. There should be performance linked pay against MoU targets and their impartial evaluation. Central Public Enterprises should be approached for their help for revival of chronically ill state enterprises. In this regard, experiment in Kerala is worth complimenting.

Ailment and Remedies

Calibrated reforms and policy measures should be undertaken for improving performance of SLPEs on the lines adopted for CPSEs by the Central Government.

Corporate Governance in SLPEs is a pre-requisite for improving managerial and control system. Good Corporate Governance, Recruitment Policy and HR Policy are essential for good governance in SLPEs. Day-to-day interventions of the government need to be restricted and they should be run by professional Board of Directors. Selection of CMDs, Independent Directors and Functional Directors should be done in a transparent manner. Moreover, CMDs/Directors of SLPEs should be given a fixed period of tenure to perform optimally. Hence, empowerment and professionalization of the Board with greater financial and functional autonomy as being extended to CPSEs could be replicated for SLPEs in order to revitalize and strengthen them further.

MoU System has proved as a very good step for increasing productivity in PSEs. It has been quite successful in encouraging and promoting excellence in overall performance of PSEs. Similarly, if State Governments also take similar steps of introduction of MoU system, it would be of great help in putting SLPEs on higher growth paths. States namely Madhya Pradesh, Karnataka, Andhra Pradesh, Delhi, Odisha, Rajasthan and Punjab have already adopted MoU system.

Introduction of Ratna concept for SLPEs, and also encouraging them to get listed on Stock Exchanges, will improve their performance and they will be able to play a more valuable role in sustainable growth of State economies. Besides, where the domain of business is same or similar for the SLPEs and CPSEs in a State, it would be important to bring about greater cohesion through constant and periodic co-ordination between them making the deliverables more effective.

Training ensures improved performance for capacity building of employees with additional skills and competencies. To improve the performance of SLPEs there is a need to look into their working and training need assessment in SLPEs. There is also need to identify and tie up with reputed Institutes of State level and Central PSEs for providing the desired learning and development modules.

The National Survey on SLPEs brought out by DPE is a major step and would facilitate the government to assess the performance of these enterprises and initiate reforms to improve the performance of SLPEs so that they can contribute much more to the growth of the country.

PSEs whether promoted by Central Government or State Government, need to continuously strive for improving efficiency, becoming increasingly competitive and adopting state-of-the-art technology to bring greater benefits to the society at large.

It is pertinent to mention that over the years Central PSEs have demonstrated that they can fight the challenges of MNCs, be globally competitive companies, improve their financial performance while remaining true to the public cause they were set up to achieve. It is time for State Level PSEs to demonstrate the same. SLPEs should adopt the CPSE model to make their organizations more market savvy, getting listed on stock exchange and create a healthy net worth for their enterprises.

ENERGY SECURITY AND PETROL

Oil and gas plays a dominant role in the economy of India and for energy security. Crude production in the country is of the order of around 38 MMT whereas import of crude is a little over 184 MMT. This has serious adverse effect on our economy. Our total export earnings in 2012-13 was around $300 billion whereas foreign exchange outgo on import of crude itself was $169 billion which is around 56% of our total export earnings. Meaning thereby, import of oil has significant negative contribution over 10% on our GDP. In the absence of possibility of major domestic discovery coming out in the near future, the proportion of import is likely to go still higher. As per one of the estimates, it will be more than 95% by 2020. This is probably the most serious issue attracting the attention of policy-makers, exporters and producers of petroleum and petroleum products. This is a serious threat to energy and economy of the country.

Natural gas sector is also not far away from problems facing the economy of the country. The present supply is about 134 million standard cubic meter per day (MMSCMD) against a demand of over 300 MMSCMD. The supply has come down substantially because of less production of natural gas by Reliance Industries Ltd (RIL). Gas supply from domestic resources has not increased substantially and increase has come out of import of **Liquefied natural gas** (LNG) against the expense of foreign exchange. Ironically, the pipeline capacity in the country exists for transportation up to 300 MMSCMD (at Appendix - III). The entire Asian market is facing deficit scenario as they have to depend on import for many years to come.

Energy is the most essential ingredient to ensure the well-being and prosperity of a nation's people. It is the essential building block for industrial and economic activity. It is not possible to imagine how a country can grow or prosper without continued supply of requisite energy to meet the needs of its economy. In India, there has been a growing concern for availability of primary commercial energy to meet the country's growth imperatives. Though Indian economy has slowed down recently due to the global economic crisis, it is still projected to become the 2nd largest economy of the world by 2050. Such growth requires a corresponding increase in the sources of energy as well as in supply infrastructure. Under these circumstances, the requirement of adequate and reliable energy supply at economic prices for optimal and inclusive growth of the country is a prime concern today. In the Indian scenario, Primary energy consumption in the last few decades has risen sharply from 100 Mtoe in 1980 to over 7 to 8 times now. The compounded average growth rate of energy consumption for the last decade has been 6.1% against the world average of 2.7%. This obviously reflects the rising economy and better socio-economic development in the country. At the same time, we are just 5% of the world energy consumption placed at 12.5 billion ton of oil equivalent. Even though we are 4th largest consumer of energy, the per capita energy consumption is very low somewhere at 466Kgoe/per capita against the world average of 1780Kgoe. The main reason being, that we have a very large population with limited resources. With 17% of the world population, we have hardly 0.8% of the world oil and natural gas resources. Even today our access to energy in the rural area is little over 40% only.

In India, our primary energy basket comprises mainly of Coal, Oil and Gas which contribute almost 93% towards energy input. Coal is around 53% and Oil and Gas are together around 41%. Coal will continue to play its dominance in energy sector because of its availability factor in spite of the fact that there is lot of hassle in coal mining and handling. On the other hand, price volatility of oil and expected global short supply may not find faster growth of oil in the energy basket but gaseous fuels particularly Natural Gas is likely to play an increased role because of its inherent physio-chemical properties and being a clean and efficient energy source. Though Natural Gas is a late comer in the energy map of our country, the rate of its growth in the last one decade has been phenomenal. Even globally, the emergence of gas as a source of primary energy is evident from the fact that it has been one of the fastest growing amongst all sources of Fossil energy. The proven reserve of Gas over the last decade has been truly phenomenal, mainly due to the emergence of unconventional gas resources and new conventional discoveries in East Africa and Brazil.

Globally, the natural gas era has truly begun during the last decade. Integration of Global Gas Markets has by far been the most significant development with cross-border gas trade becoming a Hobson's choice for gas producers who aspire to achieve assured business growth. Global gas markets are fast integrating, the commercial models are undergoing rapid changes and the market structures are evolving and fast changing. More importantly, the Asian gas markets are leading the growth in global gas sector, with special investment focus on countries like India and China.

The spiralling oil prices and the uncertainty on the pricing front are bottlenecks in the gas markets.

As liberalization progresses and the quest for energy intensifies, trading opportunities are also expanding. International gas trade accounted for 1033bcm in 2006, 31% of worldwide gas consumption. This has opened up a whole new range of possibilities – on a global scale. The gas industry is growing on global basis as demand expands and new technologies create new ways of servicing markets. Pipelines and LNG tankers are rapidly evolving to link markets previously isolated by geography.

The Asian markets would provide the major platform for growth in the global gas sector. Asia today accounts for 71% of the total LNG consumed; natural gas accounts for less than 5% of China's primary energy consumption against 9% in India. These two countries today account for around 6% of the global gas consumption which is likely to go up around 20% of the total global natural gas consumption by the year 2025.

In the absence of any major cross-country pipeline interconnections, the demand for gas in Asia will be met mainly through LNG imports. The fast growing mode for gas market integration—LNG—has mainly been interregional. Trans-national gas pipelines have continued to play a dominant gas supply option, especially between contiguous nations. LNG, however, is now gradually globalizing and LNG trading patterns are diversifying greatly. In recent times, it has been one of the key drivers of linking diverse markets and it accounts for about 32% of the global gas trade today.

Thus Asian LNG Demand is expected to remain robust and almost double at the end of this decade. There is also a fast growing spot market in Asia. The total spot and short term LNG market worldwide stood at 73.5 MMTPA, which is 31% of the total LNG traded. Asian buyers consumed 72% of all spot LNG in 2012, and just Japan, Korea and India alone consumed 61% of the total traded volume. At the same time, new market growth centres are emerging in Asia beyond the traditional demand centres of Japan, Korea and Taiwan. China imported 14.8 MMTPA and India 14 MMTPA in 2012 showing a growth of 13% and 9% respectively on a year on year basis. India and China represented a combined 12% market share of world LNG in 2012. Developments in terms of capital cost reduction and the expansion of LNG tanker trade would also complement the growth of inter-regional gas flows. In recent years, a key factor that has turned the tide for global gas markets is the prospect of America's energy independence in the near future due to emergence of Shale Gas. As a result, America is emerging as a key export source for LNG shipments around the world at competitive prices.

Talking of India, its economy is expected to show a consistent growth over the medium and long term. Its population is growing and rate of urbanization is rising fast. In the next two decades, energy requirement would grow by 3 to 4 times. LNG is playing an important role in meeting this demand. In recent years, consumption of natural gas in India has witnessed a phenomenal growth. Because of the increasing demand-supply gap in the domestic gas sector, India has emerged as one of the large importers of LNG. Today, LNG meets almost 30% of total domestic demand for gas. Further, there is a large scope for growth in gas consumption in India since the current share of gas in its energy basket is only 10%. India's energy mix is evolving and there is a clear trend towards rising share of gas. Between 2005 and 2010 gas consumption in India showed a CAGR of around 12%.

The Indian natural gas market has gone through a number of changes, which have helped attract investments and catalyse new demand and supply. The natural gas supply infrastructure in India is fast developing. Over and above, Dahej LNG regasification plant, new LNG Re-gasification facilities at Dabhol and Kochi besides 3 or 4 additional on land and floating terminals are envisaged. The current length of trunk gas pipelines in the country is around 16000kms which is expected to grow more. This will lead to an integrated National Gas Grid across the country. Gas sector alone would require around 50 billion US Dollars over the next few years in the entire gas value chain in India. In view of this, Government policies are evolving, regulators are in place and competition is increasing in upstream, midstream and downstream segments of the industry and alignment of customers towards a market determined pricing is happening.

Regulations Need Fresh Look

Current regulation under the Petroleum and Natural Gas Regulatory Board (PNGRB) requires review with respect to i) empowerment, ii) Gas Act, iii) performance since inception, and iv) restructure/remodelling to meet the basic objectives. Experience worldwide indicates that regulatory regime has gradually been evolved and enrichment has come only depending upon nature of market, support from government and industry.

In India, empowerment and clarity is the key factor with respect to functioning of the board. Besides this, producers, transporters and the Board have to act in tandem to mutually supplement the effort at least for the first five years. Unfortunately, in India there has been no serious effort in this direction and, therefore, there is need to relook and review for better functioning of the Petroleum and Natural Gas Regulatory Board.

Success of Regulatory Board would depend upon consensus and unanimity among legislatures, executives and industry. There is general talk that sufficient empowerment has not been given to the board so far by the administrative ministry and there is need for immediate re-looking into the reasons for the same and take remedial measures without further delay. Also, the board has to make its objective clear and retrospect itself whether it has really met efforts in line with world's best practices. Whether they have been able to prevent discriminatory preferential services? Whether they could prevent inefficient and unfair pricing? Whether wasteful duplication of facilities has been prevented? Whether safety norms have been followed and environmentally sound energy infrastructure as per government policy has been created? Whether the customers' interest has been protected based on the principle of equity? How many orders the board has issued so far to ensure adherence of such code? Probably there would be disappointment if we really assess the situation based on the above parameters.

Growth of City Gas Distribution (CGD) has been rather slow after the Regulatory Board came into effect from October 2007. Prior to formation of the board, a number of joint ventures came into being and cities were added for supply of Piped Natural Gas to domestic (PNG) and Compressed Natural Gas to transport (CNG) sector. Incidentally new cities could not be added after the formation of the board even though few Cities have been authorized but actual supply has not started as yet in the absence of gas resource. With this speed, probably it will take years and years to reach the goal of putting 230 cities on city gas distribution map and, therefore, special attention is required from the board for taking the benefit of natural gas to the rural areas which is in line with the vision of inclusive growth. A CNG corridor for India is also a distant dream. These are required for our better economy.

Probably India has to learn from a similar situation that prevailed earlier in the US during the mid-seventies. The year 1978 experienced a peak of gas supply shortage in the US and a Legislation of Natural Gas Policy Act (NGPA) was enacted as a part of National Energy Act (NEA) to protect consumers from the hazards of monopoly. The objectives of the act included: i) Single national natural gas market, ii) allowing market forces to establish wellhead price and iii) eliminating mismatch of supply and demand. Probably India needs micro analysis of the prevailing situation and should immediately go for Technical Advisory wing to the board/ government for the growth of gas industry.

Price is the key issue today in the Indian gas market. As many as fifteen prices are prevailing. Consumers are in stage of utmost confusion and are subjected to coercion while finalizing the long-term gas purchase contracts. In the Indian regulatory regime, the wellhead price is not under the purview of the board which is quite in line with the international practice. But at the same time, the government cannot be kept away from the responsibility of settling wellhead price in the interest of the consumers. As early as in 1940, the Supreme Court in the US had considered that those wellhead prices are subject to government oversight—if the producers and the pipeline are affiliated companies. The spirit being that it cannot be left to the sweet will of the producer to give favourable treatment to their affiliates.

In no case, the producer should be permitted to be transporter or supplier as the same would lead to monopolistic trend. We should not allow a situation to come when consumers are subjected to receive the feedstock/ fuels at different price and compete for the finished product in the open market. As a matter of fact, such a situation is prevailing in India at present. Therefore, there is no harm if PNGRB, *suo moto* takes up the cause of price fixation aspect for the sake of growth of gas industries.

Pooled Price/One Price of Gas

Natural gas pricing in India is heterogeneous and complex in nature. Probably, India is the only country where 15 different types of basic prices of gas are prevailing. It would be worth mentioning that worldwide, a single uniform benchmark price is the prevailing practice in different countries like the US (Henry Hub), the UK (National Balancing Point) and Europe (Zubreggedude index). Complexity in the pricing of natural gas in India has resulted in enormous problems with all the three players—namely producers, sellers and consumers of natural gas. Consumers have been subjected to inequitable situations because they buy their requirement of natural gas at different prices and finally compete for their finished products in the open market. This in turn creates regional imbalance for market development for natural gas. In a country where the days of matured market of natural gas are still a far cry, there is an immediate need for a single benchmarked price of natural gas.

Historically price of gas has witnessed three distinct eras. Prior to 1987, it was negotiated price broadly guided by replacement of alternative fuel, linkage being mainly with coal. The year 1987 saw the first structured pricing order on cost plus basis. Subsequent to pricing orders by Kelkar Committee (1991), Shankar Committee (1997) and finally by the Government in 2005, the idea of market driven price evolved. The second era on pricing could be linked to prices based on Production Sharing Contracts (PSC) which came as a consequence to the New Exploration and Licensing Policy (NELP). Prices emerging out of buyer-seller contracts for LNG saw yet the third pricing regime. However, the price of LNG in the international market fluctuated a lot and in order to protect the customers – particularly the power plants – we arrived at pooled prices for certain period.

As of today, different prices of natural gas prevailing in the country can be put broadly under three categories. Out of about 140 MMSCMD presently being supplied, almost 40% is based on Administered Pricing Mechanism (APM). Even in case of APM gas, there are six different prices prevailing such as $1.97/MMBTU (Power and Fertilizer), $1.18 (North Eastern Power and Fertilizer), $1.42 (North Eastern City Gas), $2.36 (Small Consumers and CGD), $2.46 (power plant in Rajasthan) and also at $4.75 (gas purchased at higher cost but sold at APM price). To add to such complexity, seven more types of prices are prevailing for gas coming out of Production Sharing contracts – be it from PMT, RAVVA, KG basin and other fields. The third category is LNG which is broadly available at prices based on buyer-seller relations largely governed through pooled price mechanism decided by Government to take care of comparatively high price of imported gas. Leave aside the gas purchased from a spot LNG market which has ranged from $6 to even $22/MMBTU.

Under the circumstances, the immediate need of the hour is to develop single benchmarked price of natural gas in India that will be in the largest interest of producers, suppliers and consumers, and also benefit the market development of natural gas in this country. The pooled price concept decided by the Government in case of LNG has given a good indicator for bringing a simple solution to this complex issue for a period at least for five years or till the time it reaches market maturity.

It appears that pooled price option has come to stay in India for a long time. This development has also given insights that can help us to arrive at a uniform single price of natural gas based on pooling mechanism. At present about 55 MMSCMD gas is APM priced ranging from $ 1.12 to $ 2.5 / million BITU and balance (about 80–85 million cu.m. of gas) is priced in between $3.02 to $5.65/million BITU. The price discovered for KG basin gas by the Empowered Group of Ministers is $ 4.2/million BITU and it accounts for about 40 MMSCMD of gas and now going down which is around 30% of the total gas supplied. Again, a single price based on pooling mechanism is probably the answer for current complexity. Selling 52 MMSCMD (APM) gas at $ 4.2 / MMBTU would fetch an additional corpus of over Rs.11000 crore annually, whereas balance quantity of about 80–85 MMSCMD of gas (if sold at $ 4.2/MMSCMD) would require adjustment of Rs. 7000 crore out of the above corpus annually to keep a single stable price of $ 4.2/MMBTU for all the gas consumers. Therefore, a balance surplus of around Rs. 4000 crore shall still be available which can be kept either for future pooling for a stable single price for five years or so. Out of this surplus, some portion could be passed on to those producers of APM gas to meet their ongoing demand of higher price. This is only a concept as the equation will depend on the final price and supply quantity which are likely to be more than present concept in future. Gas pooling will support single gas price in the country which will bring stability and help the market development of natural gas in the country and also provide much needed comfort for many gas customers. Probably, this is the answer for all the ongoing issues related to pricing of gas including litigations. There is no doubt that such a simple solution for a benchmarked price will require micro-economic studies for fine tuning before we arrive at a single price for natural gas in India. Also, such a single benchmarked price in the country would require an executive order to avoid future litigation. Policy-makers should act fast.

Equitable and Sustainable Growth

Natural gas plays an important role to strike a balance between the three objectives of sustaining high growth, security of energy supply and environmental goals which is challenging task for the developing economy of India. It is a fact that economic growth cannot be compromised. However, the benefits of greater wealth must be distributed across the length and breadth of the country's population. When the policy of liberalization and opening up of our economy started in 1991, it was hoped that it would provide higher incomes and better living standards for every citizen. However, today we find that this has not happened. There are millions of people in India who live below $1 a day. Hence the current widespread recognition and focus on inclusive growth. The human development index has hovered around 1.4% in the last 30 years even though our GDP growth rate has been high at different stages including double digit figures in the past. The Government, policy makers and industry have to focus on giving growth a human face.

One of the important ways to do so is to make energy widely available and bridge the urban and rural divide in access to basic energy services. At present $1/3^{rd}$ of India's population does not have access to electricity. Only 80% in urban and 40% in rural India have access to electricity. Over

2.6 billion people still rely on primitive fuels like forest wood and biomass for cooking and household fuel. The resulting human exposure to pollution is a major cause of ill-health in the developing and under-privileged world. A greater penetration of gaseous fuels such as gas, LPG, CNG, etc., in retail and city gas projects such as piped gas for households and CNG for automotive fuels can be quite useful in reducing health-hazards from such pollution. Thus gas is coming out as an important policy element in achieving equitable and sustainable economic growth through providing access to modern energy services to industries and people alike. Integrating entire country on pipeline network would be the need of the hour for socio-economic growth.

More importantly, a transition away from biomass fuels reduces the need to withhold children, especially girls, from school to help with domestic duties, such as fuel collection. This can not only promote gender equality but also empower womenfolk. Clean and efficient home-fuels allow women more time for leisure or income-generating pursuits by freeing them up from collecting fuel, cooking, and cleaning, etc. It ensures lower risks to their health while lowering emissions of climate-changing pollutants. Further, degradation of land due to biomass fuel gathering can be substantially reduced by supplanting the need with gaseous fuels. Thus the forest cover would also benefit due to lower impact from fuel gathering. This is a cycle of self-sustaining and highly beneficial measures which can go a long way in improving the standard of living and quality of life in less developed areas.

Growth must also be sustainable for the life and eco-systems on our planet. The economic and social effects of climate change due to pollution in the energy value chain have already assumed dangerous dimensions. Because anthropogenic emissions of carbon dioxide result primarily from the combustion of fossil fuels, energy production, supply and use in its various forms has emerged at the center of the climate change debate. Atmospheric concentrations of carbon dioxide – one of the most important greenhouse gases in the atmosphere – have been increasing alarmingly in recent years. The consequences of rapidly rising GHG emissions and air pollution are severe for all forms of life on earth including humans, due to climate change and irreversible disruption of major eco-systems.

On climate change, it would be better to quote UN Report, *"Climate change is the defining human development challenge of the 21st Century. Failure to respond to that challenge will stall and then reverse international efforts to reduce poverty. The poorest countries and most vulnerable citizens will suffer the earliest and most damaging setbacks, even though they have contributed least to the problem. Looking to the future, no country - however wealthy or powerful - will be immune to the impact of global warming... ...Increased exposure to droughts, floods and storms is already destroying opportunity and reinforcing inequality. Meanwhile, there is now overwhelming scientific evidence that the world is moving towards the point at which irreversible ecological catastrophe becomes unavoidable. Business-as-usual climate change points in a clear direction: unprecedented reversal in human development in our lifetime, and acute risks for our children and their grandchildren."*

It needs no emphasis that smart energy and environmentally safe fuels should propel human development. In the near to medium term, therefore, there is a dire need to manage a transition from high polluting fuels to low polluting fuels in an energy efficient society. This is where cleaner fuels such as natural gas and renewables can play a big role.

Matter of Governance

Governance in India is perhaps the most relevant issue that we are facing today. An efficient energy sector is the foundation of sustainable and long term economic growth. Energy security is very crucial for any economy and it goes hand in hand with prosperity of the people. Effective governance of the energy sector is crucial to ensure economic and energy security of the country. There is need to review the policy and reform oil and gas sector to attract investment. Governance issues hold the key for economy.

Key Issues Facing Gas Sector

India is heavily dependent on imports to meet its oil and natural gas demand. That calls for expediting domestic exploration activities. But exploration is losing momentum in India. That is bad omen for the country's long-term energy security and sustainability of its high economic growth. The number of blocks offered for exploration has fallen from 57 in NELP-VII to 34 in NELP-IX. The number of bids has also dropped from 45 in NELP-VII to 33 in NELP-IX. Equally dismal has been the record in terms of the number of blocks awarded—from 44 to 16—and the production sharing contracts (PSCs) signed from 41 to 13 between the two NELP rounds.

We have an oversight system in place for the sector, like the petroleum and natural gas ministry, and regulatory bodies like the directorate general of hydrocarbon and the petroleum and natural gas regulatory board. To their credit, the highly risky activity of oil exploration and production was de-risked and incentivized by introducing a new exploration licensing policy (NELP) in 1999 to take advantage of public-private partnership. However, despite favourable terms and conditions given to major countries worldwide, the bidding rounds conducted so far have met with poor responses. The regulatory bodies could not identify the ailments and arrest the falling investment in E&P activities. The DGH, formed to impart unambiguous guidance and regulation to the sector, seems incapacitated under its apparent accountability to the ministry. Since its inception as an upstream hydrocarbon regulator, the role of DGH has been unclear, as it has increasingly come to be known as the government's extended technical arm for exploration and production rather than a powerful and independent upstream regulator. Distancing governance from regulation has never gained ground. Oil experts and the oil ministry shy away from taking key decisions because they fear harsh audit scrutiny and vigilance queries. Marketing and pricing incentive are also two key factors retarding the investment climate in India.

The government's integrated energy policy noted that the present upstream regulation provided by the DGH was "neither independent nor comprehensive in a technical sense" and the "current arrangement needs to be strengthened and made independent". It is essential, therefore, to strengthen DGH and fortify it with an army of seasoned, experienced and senior functionaries to make the process of decision making quantitatively better but also transparent and objective.

The role of PNGRB as a downstream regulator for the oil and gas sector also needs strengthening and empowerment. PSCs between the government and contractors (private and public) have been a matter of concern. The contracts were conceptualized for aggressive exploration and production in a sector where any business is of high-risk nature, in the physical, commercial and political senses. Furthermore, as we delve deeper into the finer details of the PSCs, under one significant stipulation, marketing rights of the product were to rest with the contractor. In reality, however, by some unspoken code, the same marketing rights are vested in the government, which is free to choose its customers in the name of gas utilization policy. Thus, in a very delicate manner, the contractors are immensely dis-incentivized, even though some might rightly argue that government intervention is called for as the gas market is not mature enough to let market forces play.

Many aspects of PSCs call for better scrutiny and revision. Procedural delays and the final exploration licence culminating years after signing the contract, to the unavailability of accurate and freely accessible data on the acreage are key factors in bidding decisions. There are many technical and administrative glitches. For example, the exploration blocks offered for bidding were not of the size expected by and acceptable to international bidders. Establishment of E&P and archival database is required to offer blocks through the Open Acreage Licensing Policy.

The path to reform is clearly visible. Strengthening the DGH through greater autonomy, fostering a conducive environment to investments through taxation policies and more stability in RBI's monetary policies are some of the obvious reform-oriented measures in this respect. Reducing complexities in the pricing structure of fuels is also a very potent tool to attract investors. The petroleum sector is a hot bed for controversies. Exhaustive policy review is needed to introduce a system-oriented framework that is less dependent on human discretion.

Way Forward

Over regulations, less flexibility, lack of incentive and taxation relief, remunerative price combined with indecisiveness have undermined, disappointed and frustrated the entire sector. Simply speaking, governance in the energy sector refers to a set of rules and regulations. Their performance is monitored to achieve the ultimate goal of sustainable energy security. Thus higher energy security is one of the core objectives of Energy governance.

Without the right governance frameworks in energy sector, inflow of the needed scale of domestic and foreign investment would remain a distant dream. Creation of infrastructure to ensure continued and uninterrupted supply of energy to the people, industries, agriculture, services and manufacturing sectors would also be hampered. Thus, a proper framework of laws, policies, regulations and other structures is needed to channel the needed investments and infrastructure in the energy sector. This is important to enable domestic resource sufficiency and continuous energy supplies across the economy. A question arises that are we able to provide Energy Governance frameworks, which meet the desired objectives? This is especially in the context that 40% of the world's population today uses biomass and forest wood to meet its cooking needs and 20% of the world population does not have access to electricity.

In terms of the three pillars of Sustainable growth, we are short of achieving balanced economic prosperity, being environmentally responsible or achieving wider good for the people. At the same time, it is also necessary to manage the limited resources in an optimal way to ensure sustainable energy security by way of energy conservation. To sustain and support economic growth in India, energy supplies of 4-5 times may be required by 2030 or so. For this we need investments in energy resources, and development of infrastructure and institutional capability to manage growth.

There has not been any significant step up in the crude oil reserves and production in the last decade though there is some promise held out by recent Oil discovery in Barmer in Rajasthan. At the current level of consumption, proven reserves of oil as well as gas are expected to last for less than 30 years. We import around 80% of our Oil consumption. Thus sufficiency of domestic Oil and gas resources and maintaining their uninterrupted availability is a critical issue. At the same time, there is a large potential for profitable future exploration and we need to expand our domestic Oil and Gas resource base. Only around 44% of the Indian sedimentary area has been explored well so far. Investments and infrastructure in midstream and downstream parts of the value chain also require significant ramp-up.

Energy markets are such that their effective functioning cannot entirely be addressed by businesses alone. Governments, regulators, intergovernmental cooperation, dialogue, and foreign policy play a big role. Since Energy markets are increasingly international in nature, geopolitics plays a key role in their functioning. The markets can address some of these issues but the basic building blocks have to be provided by the Governments, especially in the context of developing and underdeveloped economies, which is true for

India. Also, sound and transparent energy sector governance is necessary for social and economic development. Adequate supply, reducing import dependence and incentivizing the sector is the way forward.

What is the present state of Governance in India?

Numerous policy reforms over the past 20 years have shifted India's energy sector from a predominantly government-owned system to one gradually based on market principles to certain extent. It offers a more level playing field for both public and private sectors; however, political complexity, complex structures and socio-economic disparity hindered the complete liberalization of India's energy sector.

We look at energy at present through a somewhat fragmented prism. There are, for instance, several entities and departments involved in energy sector—several ministries, sectoral regulators other departments. The mechanism to provide petroleum and fertilizer subsidy requires a more effective and targeted approach. Time has come now to implement the Integrated Energy Policy as a way forward.

The challenges in energy sector require our PSEs to source oil and gas from abroad, to have access to latest energy technologies and to invest significant amounts in creation of energy infrastructure. This is possible only if we have effective governance by Autonomous Boards of Public Sector Enterprises in India. Only then can we create truly global energy companies which can compete in the global energy market and advance India's energy security objectives.

Thus the way forward shall also be:

- Clear ownership policy and accountability of owners.
- Separation of ownership and management must be exercised so that PSEs do not remain as extended arms of administrative Ministries.
- Ownership should not transgress into the managerial domain. Balance between autonomy and control.
- Evaluation of Board and owner with respect to their accountability.

- Single window vigilance administration.
- Succession planning.
- Corporate Social Responsibility and Environmental protection.
- Faster clearance of projects.

One of the way forwards and potential areas of interest in the coming years is the use of non-petroleum transportation fuels in the transport sector. Vehicles powered by gaseous fuels such as CNG, LPG and hydrogen-gas blends displace consumption of conventional fuels such as gasoline and diesel. This not only improves our energy security by reducing our dependence on imported oil but also public health and the environment by reducing harmful emissions. Until hydrogen vehicles and fuels become commercially viable, there will be need for alternative fuels as transitional fuel. Advancing gaseous fuels technology today can also aid the transition to a future transportation network based on hydrogen fuel cells. However there is a need for an unprecedented level of expenditure on development of new infrastructure. Urgent and significant investment is essential if India is to increase supply and improve demand-side efficiency to meet its growing energy needs. The market for gaseous fuels will grow side by side with a fair, transparent and consistent regulatory and policy framework to attract the necessary investment. This will also give a boost to cross-border trade in natural gas and other fuels. It is necessary that governments, the private sector and financial institutions work together, partner and collaborate to create conditions to facilitate investment to build the necessary infrastructure.

Way Forward through Frontiers of Technology

The underlying driver creating many of the new opportunities is, of course, rapidly developing technology. A major driver behind the growth in demand for gaseous fuels such as

LNG and CNG has been the lowering of costs resulting from technological advances. There are several technologies on the near horizon, which could lead to significant new business patterns. Gasification of Solid fuels is one such area. *Gasification technologies represent the next generation of solid-feedstock-based energy production systems. The commercialization of gasification-based processes for the conversion of carbon-based feedstocks to a flexible combination of electricity, steam, fuels, chemicals, and hydrogen can lead to gasification-based processes which are more economically attractive, have higher thermal efficiencies, and demonstrate superior environmental performance compared to competing technologies.*

On the domestic front there are various matters that need greater thought such as regulatory process, development of national gas grid, roll-out of City Gas Distribution (CGD) projects, infrastructure status for gas pipelines, institutional support to diversify the usage of gas and pricing of gas, etc.

Major Issues and thrust areas awaiting Government consideration are:

1. Declared Good Status for Natural Gas for tax benefits to end users.
2. Incentivizing the taxation issues.
3. Promotion of end use applications like gas-based geysers, gas-based co-generation, gas-based heaters, etc.
4. Gas distribution policy and concerns of NELP producers.
5. Single Uniform Natural Gas Price instead of multiple and heterogeneous prices.
6. Opportunities outside India.
7. New LNG terminals.
8. Option for setting up FSRUs (Floating Storage Regasification Unit) at suitable locations need to be explored.

9. Reduction in customs duty on LNG imports.
10. Single grid tariff.
11. National Gas Grid and cross-country pipelines

Journey Forward

Often termed as the fuel of the future, gas is rather the "Fuel of the Present". The dominant global energy issues are shifting. In what is becoming a hydrocarbon-limited and carbon-constrained world, the main focus is now on energy security and sustainable growth. The developed nations must offer a supportive hand to the developing nations and enable transfer of technology in the areas of energy efficiency and conservation, carbon capture and sequestration, gasification of solid fuels especially Coal, and other connected technologies which can ensure an eco-friendly and fast economic growth for nations around the world.

Going forward, we can address six main challenges to create well-functioning infrastructure in India's energy market:

i) With the right policies, we can create global Private and National Oil and Gas Companies of India. Greater managerial autonomy and freedom to operate based on market analysis and economic deliberations.
ii) Greater intra-ministerial and inter-governmental (between central and state governments) coordination.
iii) Evolve effective pricing mechanism to incentivize producers for demand-side management and facilitate a rational allocation of resources along the value-chain by the Government.
iv) An enabling policy incentive to attract investment to meet India's growing energy demand.
v) Pursue Integrated Energy Policy to facilitate the achievement of energy policy objectives.

vi) Inform, involve and engage the people for their participation with wider policy support.

We need to ensure that India and other developing nations are able to make a smooth transition into a clean and efficient energy economy. The next decade and beyond should be very exciting for our country for the development of its Gas, LPG, CNG, CBM and related sectors. A strengthened gas sector in turn will ensure a strengthened economy.

PART - III

Untold Story of Public Sector Enterprises

Untold Story of Public Sector Enterprises in India

Governance and deliverables in PSEs are not better than the general governance prevailing in the country, which is undoubtedly at a poor stage. Better governance in turn is intertwined with corruption free, transparent and ethical values and practices in the enterprise through quality leadership in PSEs. Unfortunately, even though we have some of the best leaders in PSEs, but we have poor leadership (Refer Part-II of this Book). The owner escapes responsibility by way of keeping ownership policy vague and confusing and at the same time provides passive ownership to influence decision making both formally and informally because of extraneous considerations and socio-political compulsions. Simultaneously, the Board structure is also similar in the absence of clear-cut Board policy. Board meetings with an insufficient number of independent directors are held. Some of the Boards have no independent directors at all. The casual approach in organising Board meeting is also evident from the fact that Board Agendas come at short notice, against regulations of the Companies Act. Board's prime concern is to provide suitable vision, strategy and implementation of programmes by top-down management. It is rather ritualistic to coin a Vision Statement. Information is generally not shared by CEO with colleague directors and similarly by directors with their management team. This, in turn, creates a big gap within the enterprise, going against the principles of governance. As far as deliverables are concerned, the least said is better, so much so that because of poor governance only 30 paise out of one rupee reaches to the end beneficiary, as remarked by one of our former Prime Ministers.

CEOs in Central Public Sectors are largely a group of intellectual but subdued persons passing $2/3^{rd}$ of their productive time on unproductive things in the corridors of administrative ministry and before other seats of power. If "knowledge expressed is wisdom", then CEOs in CPSEs are wisdomless people as they do not come out openly with their views before the administrative ministry and the Minister. They succumb to formal and informal influences from the seats of power, even though this can't be substantiated. They also appease people in the seats of power for their peaceful survival. Lick up and kick down is the general mind-set. Subordinates become victims as they are subjected to their pent-up anger emanating from stress and strain. Continuous stress and strain that they experience and carry is reflected in job performance affecting day-to-day functioning in office. It adversely affects the health of a majority of CEOs in the form of hypertension and diabetes. Probably these are the reasons that the new generation is not opting for jobs in PSEs and productivity is likely to be adversely affected after 5 to 10 years. It may also be mentioned that PSEs are best for capacity building as the employees are subjected to wider exposure to diverse natures of jobs contrary to one job expertise in private sectors.

They are addicted to foreign tours and lured by awards conferred by various agencies and come out with their photographs for projecting and promoting themselves. Award giving agencies take advantage of the prevailing situation as winning awards are directly proportional to the amount of sponsorship for such events. If you look into the last five years and examine the same, you will find that their number has increased substantially. Award giving agencies make the best of such weakness in PSEs. As Director General in SCOPE, I know about their keenness to be awarded as SCOPE has been conferring Meritorious and Excellence

Awards which are generally felicitated by the Prime Minister / President of India.

Corporate Social responsibility which has mandatory 2% of net profit contribution from PSEs is another serious area and if not implemented properly, it may result in a big issue in the times to come. Therefore, social audit is essentially required even if there may be a lot of reluctance from several quarters. Further, as all NGOs, institutions and agencies utilize this fund for corporate social responsibilities of PSEs, they should be subjected to statutory audit, including CAG and RTI so that corruption does not overtake the implementation and deliverables part of CSR. PSEs and their CEOs face continuous pressure from several quarters, including seats of power for contribution to NGOs/ agencies. Mushroom growth of NGOs without having any accountability is posing a serious problem. As they are not subjected to RTI or CAG, CSR has become a hot currency and everyone's agenda. It has become a buzzword today for consultants, NGOs, academicians and so many others for obvious reasons. Holding workshop, conferences, seminars on CSR have become order of the day.

CSR requires more serious and systematic approach. Enterprises must coin parallel vision, strategy and implementation of social responsibilities besides their normal vision for product and services. PSEs must accommodate the CSR vision with their business vision and CEOs should directly involve themselves in CSR policies. A clear cut Board's policy would eliminate undue influence from several quarters. CSR has direct relation with company's brand promotion and its culture. Incidentally, culture and brand would largely depend upon trust built-up by the companies with all the stakeholders and people at large. Trust is a perishable commodity and would require nourishing on daily basis to sustain the culture and the brand. If you are not promoting and protecting your image of being ethical, transparent and corruption free on sustained basis for the social cause, you are going to lose your international opportunities. In the domestic market also you are likely to gradually become extinct and die like dinosaur. Therefore, better align your CSR with business vision and decentralize its execution. Enterprises that have a role model image will have a future in the market.

Empowerment of PSEs has gained ground as there has been constant demand for the same. But, at the same time, it has been observed that even if power has been granted to them, they approach administrative ministry before taking decisions and seem to be strongly influenced by them. There is need to change this attitude and aptitude in PSE CEOs so that they are capable of taking decisions independently.

Procurement and placement of orders are other areas of concern. On the one hand, CEOs are required to follow the set rules of procurement, on the other pressure is generated from outside to award orders to a particular party. Sometimes they also face problems from within the organization as vested interests come into play. They are required to come out of devil and deep sea as any lapse with respect to General Finance Rule (GFR) makes their life hell, not only during their active service but also in the post-superannuation period. Corruption is the key issue associated with procurement and placement of orders. Thanks to the complex multi-layer checks and balances in the PSEs and of course RTI, CEOs are highly conscious but at the same time, there is escapist tendency and decision-making for placement of orders. Reverse auction adopted by some of the PSEs is commendable.

Succession planning, appointments of functional directors, CEOs, their extension and selection of independent Directors have become an area where due/undue influence encroaches the effectiveness of the Board leaving aside delays which take place. The process of selection is also not far from aberrations.

In order to make the book more factual and significant, I had requested several of my close friends, who are CEOs of Central Public Sector Enterprises (CPSEs), to give their insight and opinion on the current state of affairs and obstacles in day-to-day working and decision-making. A copy of my communication is in *Appendix – IV*.

Unfortunately, hardly anyone wanted to express openly. Till there is courage in the CEOs to come out with a free, frank and fearless opinion, the situation is not likely to improve. The robotic way of following the remote ballistic command must end in CPSEs.

Civil servants have great intellect and occupy positions of privilege, but are often a class of pampered, ego-driven people. Civil servants work on the philosophy of status-quo and precedence, and generally do not welcome change. Probably, that was the reason that Edmund Burke, the great British thinker wrote that if you allow civil servants to rule, people will welcome them for first few months and thereafter you will see every civil servant "hanging by the nearest lamp tower". This class of people do not wish to listen to the point of dissent from CEOs.

In the absence of a clear ownership policy, civil servants of the administrative ministries become "passive owners" and get opportunities to influence the Board, both formally and informally. Memorandum and Articles of Association signed at the time of formation of enterprise only provides broad parameters for the enterprise. After more than six decades of existence of public sector in India, there is no clear-cut ownership policy issued by the administrative ministries with respect to specific enterprises. If the same is not documented and widely circulated among all shareholders (including minority shareholders), wherefrom can evaluation of accountability of administrative ministry be done? There is lack of clarity as to what owners will provide for a successful job done by the Boards in discharging their responsibilities. Therefore, all enterprises would require clear policies with respect to the owner (administrative ministries) and the Board (of the enterprise). It is better if it comes through a Sovereign Committee of the Central Government and not through the administrative Ministries as witnessed throughout the developed countries of the world in the post-recession period.

All formal/informal words coming from administrative Ministries become diktats for compliance by the CEOs. CEOs of CPSEs in India are traditionally prone to conformance than performance. As a result, productivity suffers. As CEOs have fear of unknown for their survival and stability in the enterprise, they comply happily so that the owner sitting on the seats of power are happy with them. This, in turn, creates a lot of concealed stress and strain to the CEO which takes its toll and disturbs during service life and post-superannuation period.

Independent directors become defacto "dependable independent directors" as they are selected by administrative ministry and the Minister In-charge, even though a Search Committee exists on paper. If the names forwarded by the Search Committees are not in line, they are put on hold for indefinite period in the list till the time the Ministry forwards its choice to DOPT/ACC. As of now, around 200 posts of Independent Directors are vacant. Also half of the functional Board positions are required to be independent directors as per clause 49 of the Listing Agreement of the Securities and Exchange Board of India (SEBI), which has made the Board structure too unwieldy to manage business. Obviously, there is delay in clearing Board agenda because of large number of persons on the Board; in line with Parkinson's Law that work multiplies according to the number of people.

In the recent Companies Bill (now Act), duties and responsibilities of independent directors have been defined. Department of Public Enterprises (DPE) has also come out with a circular indicating that the non-official (independent) directors of the company shall hold at least one meeting in a year, without the attendance of functional and government directors and members of management. All the non-official (independent) directors of the company shall strive to be present at such meeting. The meeting shall review the performance of functional directors and government nominee directors and the Board as a whole. Also review the performance of the Chairperson of the company. This has also been substantiated by the government gazette notification on Companies Act, 2013. They are also supposed to assess the quality, quantity and timeliness of flow of information between the Board and company management necessary for the Board to effectively and reasonably perform their duties. This in some way will affect the autonomy of the Board as Independent Directors along with Government nominee Directors constitute the majority in the Board. Independent Directors as a class align in line with Government Nominee Directors in the Board meetings. This is rather paradoxical against the constant demand of autonomy of the Board so that ownership does not transgress into the operational and functional domains of the Board. Structure of the Board with 50% independent directors and two government nominee directors provides them majority positions in the Board to pursue any agenda (open or hidden) in the Board meetings. Also, in view of this, positions of Chairman/ functional directors have become shaky because of majority of independent Directors and Government nominee Directors in the Board. Therefore, instead of granting larger autonomy, the Boards of PSEs are under larger control of the government. PSE Boards have been reduced to the stage of extended arm of the administrative ministry. Probably this may be the reason that in the post-recession period, the Sovereign Committees without administrative Ministry is being considered in developed and developing countries, viz., Sweden, Norway, Vietnam, even Malaysia, where administrative ministry have no, or negligible say in the decision making. Such sovereign committees look into succession planning and help PSEs through Sovereign Wealth Fund (SWF). There is need for bringing further reform in the area of Corporate Governance by way of constituting an expert committee of eminent person(s) on corporate governance in PSEs. Such a committee is long due after we have had committees headed by Kumarmangalam Birla, Narayana Murthy, Naresh Chandra and J.J. Irani. The Expert Committee should take note of changing trends world over.

Information sharing between inter and intra departments is a lacking point as people in PSEs largely prefer to work in isolation. There is no system for flow of information on regular basis that does not help in team building. There is a need for information sharing mechanisms at various layers of the enterprise and performance should be evaluated against it.

CEOs who do not succumb to the pressure are subjected to larger stress/strain in one way or the other. When I was CEO of a then Navratna, now Maharatna company, I remember to attract the axe including an intended charge sheet on several occasions, but thanks to the Minister who probably did not allow. These were events when: (i) I wanted my company to purchase 5.7% equity of ADB in Petronet LNG Limited (PLL) for which I wrote a formal letter to the then Secretary; and (ii) Selecting Chairman of PLL by a Search Committee as per joint venture agreement signed at the time of formation of PLL. Incidentally, Secretary (Petroleum and Natural Gas) even today happens to be Chairman of PLL (a well-acknowledged private sector company) ignoring the concept of conflict of interest. The other occasion was when I requested for 2.5% equity of Oil India Limited (as thrown open) in favour of GAIL on the principle of equity, allocating 2.5% each to Indian Oil Corporation Limited, Bharat Petroleum Corporation Limited, Hindustan Petroleum Corporation Limited and GAIL. In spite of my sincere efforts, I lost opportunities as I was snubbed by the administrative Ministry. There were also many such occasions when I approached the owner Ministry for providing level playing field with others but all efforts were futile. There might be a large number of such occasions for other CEOs who preferred not to reply to my request letter. Such a relation with administrative Ministries has become a bottleneck for taking initiatives by CEOs.

The Nehruvian concept of Government control of public sector is being gradually diluted; as such there has been denigration of PSEs in the recent past, whereas there is also a continuous demand for selling larger equity in the hands of private sector. I do not understand how the concept of handing over such a large capital in private hands and the objective of welfare state can go together, especially when the experience worldwide in the post-recession period has been quite different. I do not want to fall into any controversy on "capital in hands of private vs. capital in the hands of state" but definitely latter is the preferred option for public sector. It appears that the private entities prevail as usual, as they prevailed against the demand for level playing and bringing them under CAG/Vigilance Administration or RTI on equitable basis with PSEs. The argument given that RTI, CAG and similar checks and balances are for those enterprises, which hold public money and tax payers' money. Private sectors also hold public/tax payers' money on projects, which is mobilized from Banks and Financial agencies. To me, it appears that all money is public money unless it is black money.

Political economy has its own hazards. Notwithstanding all other things there is no doubt that it also retards adaptability and change management. Political system wants immediate results and cannot wait for a long time as public image is more important for them. The World Bank in one of its recent reports (2013–14) has said:

"Political economy problems hinder risk management. Even when resources are available, politicians may be reluctant to devote them to risk management because the cost of risk management are immediate, concentrated and observable, while benefits are long term, distributed more broadly and often less visible."

Convergence of the plethora of laws and regulations is essential for bringing more efficiency in the Board of PSEs. The multiple layers of checks and balances come in the way of efficient and effective decision making by the enterprises. The five 'Cs', viz. CVO, CAG, CVC, CBI and CCI, can be compared with the epic of the five Pandav brothers wed to one Draupadi (i.e. PSEs). Apprehension in the heart of PSE CEOs adversely affects productivity, efficiency and overall decision-making. Immediate reforms and correcting the present governance system is the need of the hour. Till the present state of affairs of CEOs does not change, they have no choice but to enjoy the imminent slavery.

Finally, I wish that there must be:

- Clear-cut ownership policy.
- Faster succession planning and better structure of the Board.
- Evaluation and accountability of owner and Board against benchmarked positions.
- Autonomy of the board.
- Selection of Independent Directors through impartial sovereign committee.
- Relinquishing the influence of administrative Ministry.
- Convergence by multi-layer check and balances system and regulations.
- Massive training programmes at all level.
- Developing information sharing mechanism in the organization.
- Integrity and transparency.
- Accommodating social vision with business vision.
- CEO should reflect as role model in the organization.
- Developing an organizational culture based on ethics.

Appendices

Appendix - I

List of CPSEs

Maharatna CPSEs

1. Bharat Heavy Electricals Limited
2. Coal India Limited
3. GAIL (India) Limited
4. Indian Oil Corporation Limited
5. NTPC Limited
6. Oil & Natural Gas Corporation Limited
7. Steel Authority of India Limited

Navratna CPSEs

1. Bharat Electronics Limited
2. Bharat Petroleum Corporation Limited
3. Hindustan Aeronautics Limited
4. Hindustan Petroleum Corporation Limited
5. Mahanagar Telephone Nigam Limited
6. National Aluminium Company Limited
7. NMDC Limited
8. Neyveli Lignite Corporation Limited

9. Oil India Limited
10. Power Finance Corporation Limited
11. Power Grid Corporation of India Limited
12. Rashtriya Ispat Nigam Limited
13. Rural Electrification Corporation Limited
14. Shipping Corporation of India Limited

Miniratna Category - I CPSEs

1. Airports Authority of India
2. Antrix Corporation Limited
3. Balmer Lawrie & Co. Limited
4. Bharat Dynamics Limited
5. BEML Limited
6. Bharat Sanchar Nigam Limited
7. Bridge & Roof Company (India) Limited
8. Central Warehousing Corporation
9. Central Coalfields Limited
10. Chennai Petroleum Corporation Limited
11. Cochin Shipyard Limited
12. Container Corporation of India Limited
13. Dredging Corporation of India Limited
14. Engineers India Limited
15. Ennore Port Limited
16. Garden Reach Shipbuilders & Engineers Limited
17. Goa Shipyard Limited
18. Hindustan Copper Limited
19. HLL Lifecare Limited
20. Hindustan Newsprint Limited

21. Hindustan Paper Corporation Limited
22. Housing & Urban Development Corporation Limited
23. India Tourism Development Corporation Limited
24. Indian Railway Catering & Tourism Corporation Limited
25. IRCON International Limited
26. KIOCL Limited
27. Mazagaon Dock Limited
28. Mahanadi Coalfields Limited
29. Manganese Ore (India) Limited
30. Mangalore Refinery & Petrochemical Limited
31. Mishra Dhatu Nigam Limited
32. MMTC Limited
33. MSTC Limited
34. National Fertilizers Limited
35. National Seeds Corporation Limited
36. NHPC Limited
37. Northern Coalfields Limited
38. North Eastern Electric Power Corporation Limited
39. Numaligarh Refinery Limited
40. ONGC Videsh Limited
41. Pawan Hans Helicopters Limited
42. Projects & Development India Limited
43. Railtel Corporation of India Limited
44. Rashtriya Chemicals & Fertilizers Limited
45. RITES Limited
46. SJVN Limited
47. Security Printing and Minting Corporation of India Limited

48. South Eastern Coalfields Limited
49. State Trading Corporation of India Limited
50. Telecommunications Consultants India Limited
51. THDC India Limited
52. Western Coalfields Limited
53. WAPCOS Limited

Miniratna Category-II CPSEs

54. Bharat Pumps & Compressors Limited
55. Broadcast Engineering Consultants (I) Limited
56. Central Mine Planning & Design Institute Limited
57. Ed.CIL (India) Limited
58. Engineering Projects (India) Limited
59. FCI Aravali Gypsum & Minerals India Limited
60. Ferro Scrap Nigam Limited
61. HMT (International) Limited
62. HSCC (India) Limited
63. India Trade Promotion Organisation
64. Indian Medicines & Pharmaceuticals Corporation Limited
65. M E C O N Limited
66. Mineral Exploration Corporation Limited
67. National Film Development Corporation Limited
68. National Small Industries Corporation Limited
69. P E C Limited
70. Rajasthan Electronics & Instruments Limited

Other CPSEs - Non Ratna

1. Artificial Limbs Manufacturing Corporation of India Ltd
2. Air India Ltd
3. Air India Air Transport Services Ltd
4. Air India Charters Ltd
5. Airline Allied Services Ltd
6. Bharat Bhari Udyog Nigam Ltd
7. BBJ Construction Company Ltd
8. Bisra Stone Lime Company Ltd
9. Central Inland Water Transport Corporation Ltd
10. Electronics Corporation of India Ltd
11. Karnataka Antibiotics & Pharmaceuticals Ltd
12. Hindustan Shipyard Ltd
13. National Backward Classes Finance & Development Corporation
14. Central Railside Warehousing Co. Ltd
15. Cotton Corporation of India Ltd
16. ECGC Limited
17. Food Corporation of India Ltd
18. Fertilizers & Chemicals Travancore Ltd
19. Handicrafts & Handlooms Exports Corporation Ltd
20. Hindustan Prefab Limited
21. HMT Watches Ltd
22. HMT Chinar Watches Ltd
23. Hoogly Dock & Port Engineers Ltd
24. Hotel Corporation of India Ltd
25. Indian Rare Earths Limited

26. Jute Corporation of India Ltd
27. Indian Railway Finance Corporation Ltd
28. Indian Renewable Energy Dev. Agency Ltd
29. National Handicapped Finance & Development Corporation
30. National Informatics Centre Services Inc.
31. National Buildings Construction Corporation
32. National Handloom Dev. Corporation Ltd
33. National Projects Construction Corpn. Ltd
34. National Safai Karamcharis Finance & Development Corporation
35. National Scheduled Castes Finance & Development Corporation
36. NTPC Vidyut Vyapar Nigam Ltd
37. National ST Fin & Development Corporation
38. Nuclear Power Corporation of India Ltd
39. National Research Development Corporation
40. Orissa Minerals Dev. Company Ltd
41. Rail Vikas Nigam Ltd
42. Rajasthan Drugs & Pharmaceuticals Ltd
43. State Farms Corporation of India Ltd
44. Uranium Corporation of India Ltd
45. National Minorities Development & Finance Corporation
46. HMT Ltd
47. Konkan Railway Corporation Ltd
48. Mumbai Railway Vikas Corporation Ltd
49. National Textile Ltd
50. Brahmaputra Valley Fertilizer Corporation Ltd

51. Central Electronics Limited
52. Hindustan Steelworks Construction Ltd
53. Andaman & Nicobar Island Forest & Plant Dev Corporation
54. Central Cottage Industries Corporation of India
55. North Eastern Handicrafts & Handloom Dev Corporation
56. STCL Ltd
57. Assam Ashok Hotel Corporation Ltd
58. BEL Optronics Devices Ltd
59. BHEL Electricals Machines Ltd
60. Certification Engineers International Ltd
61. Donyi Polo Ashok Hotel Ltd
62. Fresh & Healthy Enterprises Ltd
63. GAIL Gas Limited
64. Eastern Investment Ltd
65. IDPL (Tamil Nadu) Ltd
66. Indian Vaccine Corporation Ltd
67. IRCON Infrastructure & Service Ltd
68. J&K Mineral Development Corporation Ltd
69. Kanti Bijlee Utpadan Nigam Ltd
70. Karnataka Trade Promotion Organization
71. Kumarakruppa Frontier Hotels Ltd
72. Madhya Pradesh Ashok Hotel Corporation Ltd
73. NTPC Electric Supply Company Ltd
74. PFC Capital Advisory Service Ltd
75. PFC Consulting Ltd
76. Power System Operation Corporation Ltd

77. Prize Petroleum Company Ltd
78. Pondicherry Ashok Hotel Corporation Ltd
79. Ranchi Ashok Bihar Hotel Corporation Ltd
80. REC Power Distribution Co. Ltd
81. REC Transmission Project Co. Ltd
82. Tamil Nadu Trade Promotion Organization
83. Sambhar Salts Ltd
84. Utkal Ashok Hotel Corporation Ltd
85. SAIL Refractory Company Ltd
86. Millennium Telecom Ltd
87. Bharat Petro Resources Ltd
88. NHDC Limited
89. Creda HPCL Biofuels Ltd
90. HPCL Biofuels Ltd
91. Hooghly Printing Company Ltd
92. Balmer Lawrie Investment Ltd
93. Indian Infrastructure Finance Ltd

Financially Stressed CPSEs

1. Vignyan Industries Limited
2. North Eastern Regional Agriculture Marketing Corporation
3. Bharat Immunologicals & Biologicals Corporation Limited
4. Hindustan Salts Limited
5. Hindustan Insecticides Limited
6. Hindustan Organic Chemicals Limited
7. Nagaland Pulp & Paper Co. Limited

8. Biecco Lawrie Limited
9. Hindustan Vegetable Oils Corporation Ltd
10. The British India Corporation Ltd
11. Tyre Corporation of India Ltd
12. Braithwaite & Co. Ltd
13. National Jute Manufactures Corporation Ltd
14. Instruments Ltd
15. Hindustan Fluorocarbons Ltd
16. Cement Corporation of India Ltd
17. Hindustan Antibiotics Ltd
18. Eastern Coalfields Ltd
19. Bharat Coking Coal Ltd
20. Andrew Yule and Company Limited
21. Bharat Heavy Plates and Vessels Limited
22. HMT Machine Tools Limited
23. Triveni Structurals Ltd
24. Heavy Engineering Corporation Limited
25. Orissa Drugs & Chemicals Ltd
26. Hindustan Photofilms Mfg. Co. Ltd
27. Hindustan Cables Ltd
28. Indian Drugs and Pharmaceuticals Ltd
29. Scooters India Ltd
30. Richardson & Cruddas (1972) Ltd
31. Fertilizers Corporation of India Ltd
32. Hindustan Fertilizers Corporation Ltd
33. Burn Standard Co. Ltd
34. NEPA Limited
35. Birds Jute and Exports Ltd

36. Bharat Wagon & Engg. Co. Ltd
37. ITI Limited
38. Tungabhadra Steel Products Limited
39. HMT Bearings Limited
40. Madras Fertilizer Limited
41. Bengal Chemicals & Pharmaceuticals Ltd

Under Construction CPSEs

1. Air India Engineering Services Ltd
2. Bharat Broadband Network Ltd
3. Bharat Petro Resources JPDA
4. Bharat Nabhikiya Vidyut Nigam Ltd
5. Bharat Rail Bijlee Co. Ltd
6. Biotechnology Industry Research Assistance Council
7. Brahmaputra Crackers & Polymer Ltd
8. Chhattishgarh Surguja Power Ltd
9. Coastal Karnataka Power Ltd
10. Coastal Maharashtra Mega Power Ltd
11. Coastal Tamil Nadu Power Ltd
12. Dedicated Fright Corridor Corpn of India Ltd
13. Dgen Transmission Co. Ltd
14. Ghogarpalli Integrated Power Company Ltd
15. HLL Biotech Ltd
16. Indian Oil Creda Biofuels Ltd
17. Irrigation & Water Resources Finance Corporation Ltd
18. Jagdishpur Paper Mills Ltd
19. Loktak Downstream Hydroelectric Corporation Ltd
20. Mahanadi Basin Power Ltd

21. MJSJ Coal Ltd
22. MNH Shakti Ltd
23. NLC Tamil Nadu Power Ltd
24. NMDC Power Limited
25. NMDC CMDC Limited
26. NTPC Hydro Ltd
27. Orissa Integrated Power Ltd
28. PFC Green Energy Ltd
29. Power Equity Capital Advisors Pvt Ltd
30. Punjab Ashok Hotel Company Ltd
31. RITES Infrastructure Services Ltd
32. SAIL Jagadishpur Power Plant Ltd
33. Sakhigopal Integrated Power Co. Ltd
34. Sethusamudram Corporation Ltd
35. Tatiya Andhra Mega Power Ltd

Macro-View of Performance of CPSEs

(₹ in crore)

Particulars	2002-03	2003-04	2004-05	2005-06	2006-07	2007-08	2008-09	2009-10	2010-11	2011-12
	(As per Pre-Revised Schedule VI)								(As per Revised schedule VI)	
No. of operating Enterprises	226	230	227	226	217	214	213	217	220	225
Capital employed	417160	452336	504407	585484	661338	724009	792232	908007	1153947	1328027
Total Gross Turnover/ Revenue	572833	630704	744307	837295	964890	1096308	1271529	1244805	1498018	1841927
Total Net Income/Revenue	548912	613706	734944	829873	970356	1102772	1309639	1272219	1470569	1824627
Net Worth	241846	291828	341595	397275	454134	518485	583144	652993	709505	766439
Profit before dep,Impairment, Int, Exc. Items,Ex.Or. Items &taxes (PBDIEET)	101691	127320	142554	150262	177990	195049	186836	211184	219714	250438
Depreciation, Depletion & Amortization	28247	31251	33147	34848	33141	36668	36780	41603	57118	60528
DRE/Impairment	905	1025	986	992	5841	5802	7661	9565	187	154
Profit before Int, Exc. Items, Ex.Or. Items &taxes (PBIEET)	72539	95039	108420	114422	139008	152579	142395	160017	162409	189756
Interest	23921	23835	22869	23708	27481	32126	39300	36060	29724	41060
Profit before Exc. Items, Ex.Or. Items &taxes (PBEET)	48618	71144	85550	90714	111527	120453	103095	123957	132686	148696
Exceptional Items	—	—	—	—	—	—	—	—	-1479	3927
Profit before Ex.Or. Items &taxes (PBET)	—	—	—	—	—	—	—	—	134164	144769
Extra-Ordinary Items	-1225	-3933	-1075	-3192	-3880	-1570	-14600	-8264	-2786	-452
Profit before taxes (PBT)	49843	75077	86625	93906	115407	122023	117695	132221	136950	145221
Tax provisions	17499	22134	21662	24370	34352	40749	33828	40018	44871	47709
Net Profit/Loss after Tax from Continuing Operations	32344	52943	64963	69536	81055	81274	83867	92203	92079	97512
Net Profit/Loss after Tax from Discontinuing Operations	—	—	—	—	—	—	—	—	49	1
Overall Net Profit/Loss	32344	52943	64963	69536	81055	81274	83867	92203	92128	97513
Profit of profit making CPSEs	43316	61606	74432	76382	89581	91577	98488	108434	113944	125116
Loss of loss incurring CPSEs	10972	8522	9003	6845	8526	10303	14621	16231	21817	27602
Profit making CPSEs (No.)	119	139	143	160	154	160	158	157	158	161
Loss Incurring CPSEs (No.)	105	89	73	63	61	54	55	60	62	63
CPSEs Making no profit/loss	2	2	-	1	1	-	-	-	-	1
No. of Operating CPSEs that have not furnished information	—	—	—	2	1	—	—	—	—	—
Dividend	13769	15288	20718	22886	26819	28123	25501	33223	35700	42627
Dividend tax	1193	1961	2852	*3215*	4107	4722	4132	5151	5394	5877
Retained profit	17382	35835	41394	43435	50129	48429	54233	53820	51056	49009

Appendix – II

Chief Vigilance Commission

- Office Order No. 41/12/07 dated 4 December 2007
- Office Order No. 43/12/07 dated 28 December 2007
- Circular No. 18/05/08 dated 19 May 2008
- Circular No. 24/8/08 dated 5 August 2008
- Circular No. 10/05/09 dated 18 May 2009
- Circular No. 17/04/10 dated 19 April 2010
- Circular No. 06/07//12 dated 23 July 2012

Department of Public Enterprises

- Office Memorandum dated 9 September 2011

Ministry of Finance

- Office Memorandum dated 19 July 2011

Appendix – III

GAS PIPELINES IN INDIA

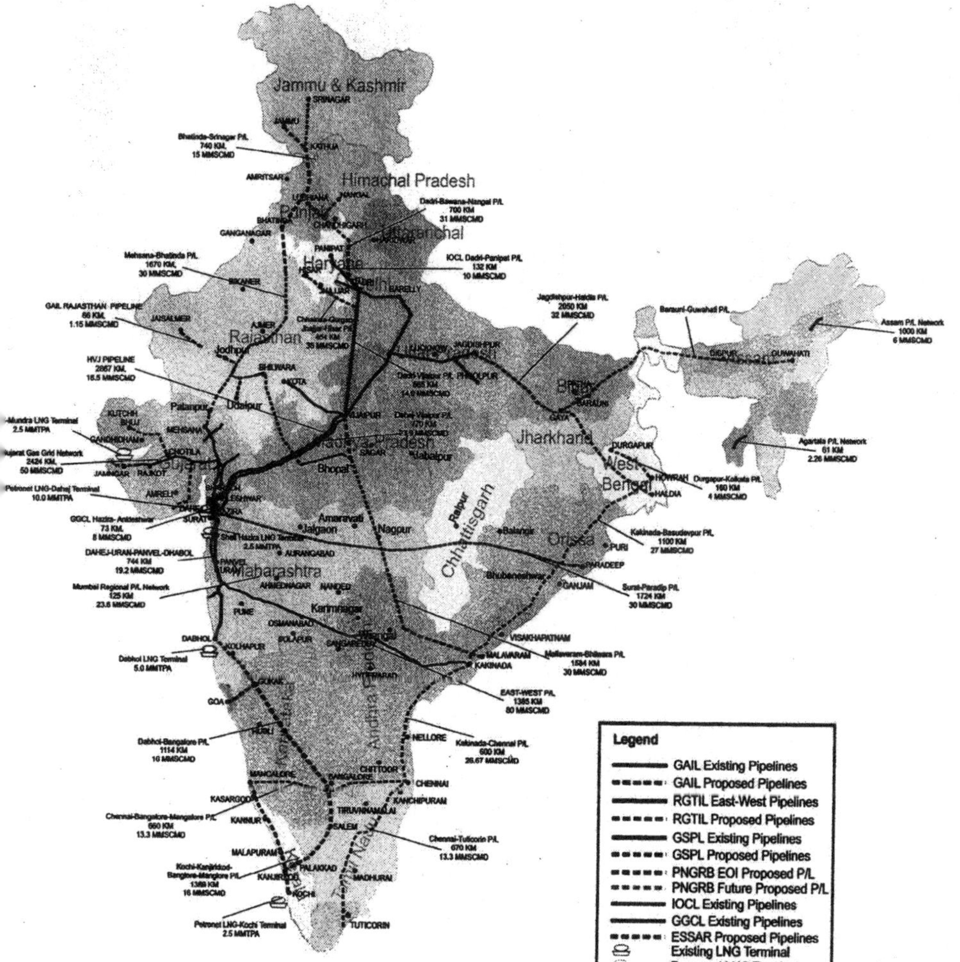

Legend

- GAIL Existing Pipelines
- GAIL Proposed Pipelines
- RGTIL East-West Pipelines
- RGTIL Proposed Pipelines
- GSPL Existing Pipelines
- GSPL Proposed Pipelines
- PNGRB EOI Proposed P/L
- PNGRB Future Proposed P/L
- IOCL Existing Pipelines
- GGCL Existing Pipelines
- ESSAR Proposed Pipelines
- Existing LNG Terminal
- Proposed LNG Terminal

- Not to the Scale
- Pipelines Route are Indicative in Nature
- Authenticity of indicated P/L may be ascertained from PNGRB

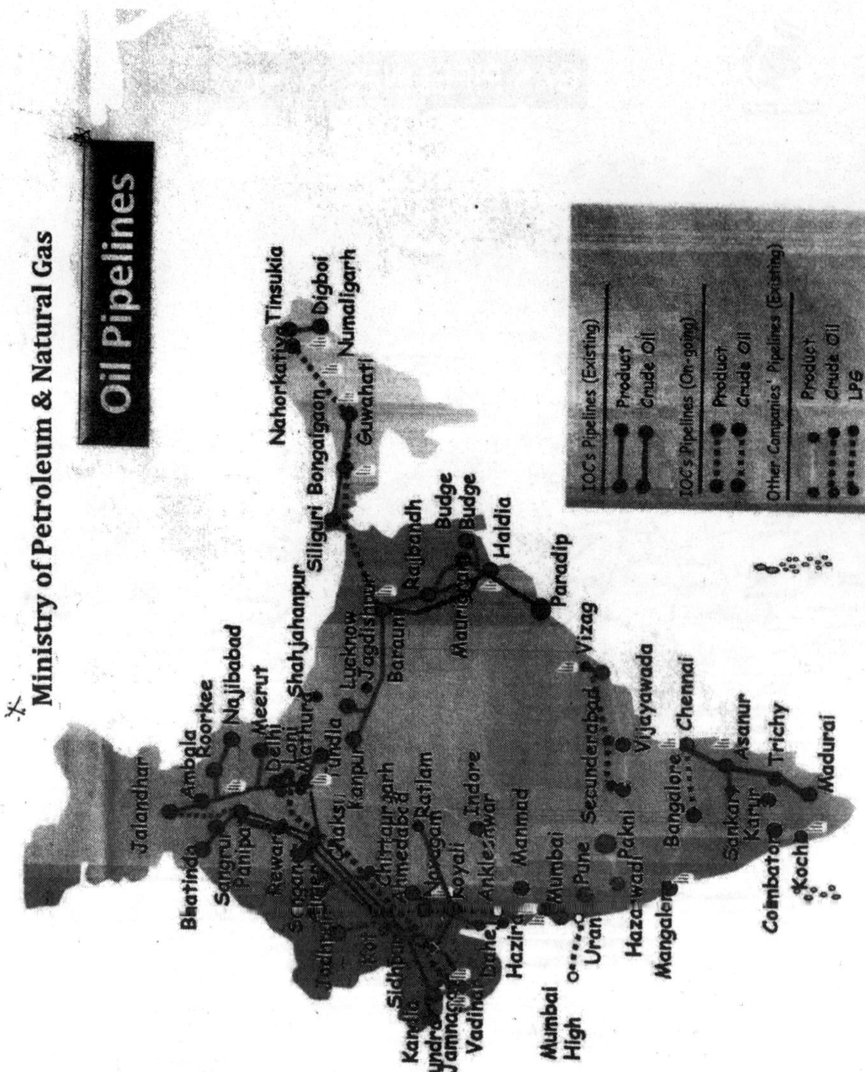
Ministry of Petroleum & Natural Gas
Oil Pipelines
IOCs Pipelines (Existing)
Product
Crude Oil
IOCs Pipelines (On-going)
Product
Crude Oil
Other Companies' Pipelines (Existing)
Product
Crude Oil
LPG
Jalandhar
Ambala
Roorkee
Najibabad
Meerut
Delhi
Bhatinda
Sangrur
Panipat
Rewari
Mathura
Tundla
Shahjahanpur
Lucknow
Kanpur
Jagdishpur
Barauni
Siliguri
Bongaigaon
Guwahati
Nahorkatiya
Tinsukia
Digboi
Numaligarh
Rajbandh
Budge Budge
Haldia
Paradip
Vizag
Vijayawada
Chennai
Secunderabad
Asanur
Trichy
Madurai
Sankari
Karur
Coimbatore
Kochi
Bangalore
Mangalore
Hazarwadi
Pune
Mumbai
Uran
Mumbai High
Manmad
Indore
Ratlam
Ankleshwar
Koyali
Navagam
Ahmedabad
Chittaurgarh
Hazira
Dahej
Vadinar
Jamnagar
Mundra
Kandla
Sidhpur
Kot
Jodhpur
Sanganer
Chaksu

Appendix - IV

Copy of Letter to CEOs

SCOPE/2012/
May 29, 2012

Dear

The objective of writing this communication to you is to seek your valuable guidance, based on your experience as CEO in Public Sector Enterprise(s). As I have started writing a research-oriented book on ***"Corporate Culture prevailing in Public Sector Enterprises in India"*** *and shall come out boldly with remedial measures so that at least future generation of CEOs have better days, not only in terms of efficiency and productivity but also a peaceful, healthy and long life after superannuation. Therefore, the first request to you would be to* ***please not pass on this paper*** *to subordinates and instead devote some time to help me complete this very important project in the larger interest of our PSEs, particularly the CEOs. This may be difficult because of your very busy schedule but you will appreciate that without your support and feedback the comments would not be complete in all respects.*

The expectations are of an honest feedback with regard to formal/informal interference by the concerned administrative Ministry at various levels, through ministers, politicians and other outside environmental influence affecting the productivity and working of the CEOs. I know that things may be a bit difficult to outrightly criticize but there is no harm if we keep the academic value above everything to bring professionalization of PSE Boards. Here, I must make it clear at this stage that wherever you want to keep the same confidential, without quoting the name, the same shall be followed but the true corporate culture should emerge once the book is published. There may be so many events which you may deem fit to inform which, in turn, will help me complete this very important task in my life. Please also come out with your suggestions to improve the corporate culture in PSEs.

It has been a matter of great concern for me because having served as CMD of a Navratna company, I got ample opportunity to reinvent/retrospect and unwind the past while lying on the hospital bed for 25 days. I realized that the plight of other CMDs are not far different than me and I must share my experience and hazards thereof to keep the CEOs in good health not only during the active service but in future, in the post superannuation period because of stress, strain, etc.

I am not giving very many details but I know you are the better judge to analyze once the objectives are clear. Therefore, I once again request you to kindly personally apply your mind and come out boldly to give feedback to the undersigned for which I shall be ever obliged.

*I request that your views may be given on my personal E-mail ID : (**udchoubey@gmail.com**). I shall be available for any further assistance in this regard.*

With regards,

Yours sincerely,
Sd/-
(Dr. U.D. Choubey)